GOOD BOY

By the Same Author

MEMOIRS

She's Not There

I'm Looking Through You

Stuck in the Middle with You

STORIES

Remind Me to Murder You Later

NOVELS

The Planets

The Constellations

Getting In

Long Black Veil

YOUNG ADULT

Falcon Quinn and the Black Mirror

Falcon Quinn and the Crimson Vapor

Falcon Quinn and the Bullies of Greenblud

NOVELLA

I'll Give You Something to Cry About

GOOD BOY

MY LIFE IN SEVEN DOGS

Jennifer Finney Boylan

CELADON
BOOKS

NEW YORK

www.celadonbooks.com

Designed by Donna Sinisgalli Noetzel

The Library of Congress has cataloged the hardcover edition as follows:

Names: Boylan, Jennifer Finney, 1958– author.
Title: Good boy : my life in seven dogs / Jennifer Finney Boylan.
Description: First edition. | New York : Celadon Books, 2020.
Identifiers: LCCN 2019037746 | ISBN 9781250261878 (hardcover) | ISBN 9781250261861 (ebook)
Subjects: LCSH: Boylan, Jennifer Finney, 1958– | Novelists, American—20th century—Biography. | Dog owners—United States—Biography. | Dogs—United States—Biography. | Human-animal relationships.
Classification: LCC PS3552.O914 Z46 2020 | DDC 818/.5403 [B]—dc23
LC record available at https://lccn.loc.gov/2019037746

ISBN 978-1-250-78349-3 (trade paperback)

First Celadon Books Paperback Edition: 2021

10 9 8 7 6 5 4 3 2 1

For Zai

Cave Canem

In a handful of instances in this book I have used pseudonyms for some of the humans, in order to protect the privacy of the dogs.

Parts of this story first appeared in very different form in *The New Yorker* and *The New York Times*. I am grateful to my editors there—Sharan Shetty, Clay Risen, and Jim Dao—for their support and patience, as well as to Deb Futter at Celadon, who edited *She's Not There* in 2003 and returns to me now like a long-lost sister.

I'm always grateful to hear from readers. My email is jb@jenniferboylan.net.

Contents

What shall I do for you, Water Strider?
Kiss the anger from your shoulders,
weave you a cape of ribbon grass
and fallen eyelashes
to protect you? Shall I transform my fingers
into quiet raindrops on your back?
I can do all this, Water Strider,
and still cradle the tidal pool
with your seahorse swimming in it
while you gently brush my hair.

—*Nancy Johnson*

GOOD BOY

Too Dark to Read

I took her picture one sparkling autumn day, as she stood in our dirt road waiting. There was a bright red maple leaf on the ground.

A year later, I held that photo in my hands as the tears rolled down. An Eva Cassidy ballad, "Autumn Leaves," played on the radio. It was an old sad song.

My children had been twelve and ten back in 2006. Our family had been through a wrenching couple of years. And yet we'd emerged on the other side of those days still together, the four of us plus Ranger, the black Lab. Our lives revolved around that dog and each other.

But we worried that Ranger felt puny when we weren't around. Sometimes we arrived back at the house to hear him howling piteously. It was heartbreaking, his loneliness.

Then, someone emailed us about this dog named Indigo. She'd had puppies a few months before, and now she needed a home. Were the Boylans interested?

The Boylans were.

Indigo joined us as Ranger's wing-dog. When she first stepped through the door, her underbelly still showed the recent signs of the litter she'd delivered. Between the wise droopy face and the swinging dog teats, she was a sight to behold.

She had a nose for trouble. On one occasion, I came home to find that she'd eaten a five-pound bag of flour. She was covered in white powder, and flour paw prints were everywhere, including, incredibly, the countertops. I asked the dog what the hell had happened, and Indy just looked at me with a glance that said, *I cannot imagine to what you are referring.*

Time passed. Our children grew up and went off to college. I left my job at Colby College in Maine and joined the faculty at Barnard. My mother died at age ninety-four. The mirror, which had reflected a young mom when Indigo first barged through the door, now showed a woman in late middle age. I had surgery for cataracts. I began to lose my hearing. We all turned gray: me, my spouse, the dogs.

That summer, I took Indigo for one last walk. She was slow and unsteady on her paws. She looked up at me mournfully. *You did say you'd take care of me, when the time came,* she said. *You promised.*

She died on an August afternoon, a tennis ball at her side.

Sometimes, in the weeks that followed, I'd find myself searching for her, as if she might be sleeping in one of my children's empty bedrooms. But she wasn't there.

What was it I was looking for, as I poked around the house? Was it really the dog I'd lost? By the time you're in your fifties, a lot of things have flown. You learn to make your peace with ghosts, but it's an uneasy truce, at best. I'd sit in my children's bedrooms now and again and get all mopey about the fact that they'd become adults so swiftly. Here were the talismans of their childhood: finger paintings from pre-K, an old soccer ball, college diplomas.

The rooms reminded me of a photograph I'd once seen of the tomb of Tutankhamun, with the relics of the boy-king's life—a golden mask, an ancient checkerboard—strewn around the burial chamber. They lay where they'd been left, three thousand years before.

I'd been their mother for seventeen years, but for years before *that* I'd been a father, a boyfriend, a child. I had never regretted coming out as trans, living in the world without shame or secrets. But there were times when I remembered my younger self the way you'd remember a dear friend you'd lost, for reasons you no longer quite understood. Where *was* that "boy," that adorable nerd who'd spent his days sitting on the banks of a stream in Pennsylvania, fishing for brook trout? I wondered, sometimes, what had become of him. Would it be necessary, in the days to come, to refer to him only in scare quotes?

My days have been numbered in dogs. Even now, when I try to take the measure of the people I have been, I count the years by the dogs I owned in each season. When I was a boy, for instance, I had a dalmatian named Playboy, a resentful hoodlum who loved no one except my father. Later, as a hippie teenager, I had another dalmatian, a mournful, swollen creature named Sausage. While I was off at Wesleyan becoming insufferably cool, my sister brought a mutt named Matt home from Carleton, a dog whose insatiable sex drive and accompanying disregard for the rule of law made it abundantly clear that he was determined, as they say in Ireland, *to live a life given over totally to pleasure.* Still later, during my years as a nascent hipster in New York, my family acquired a Lab named Brown whose only true devotion was to eating her own paws, a pastime that obsessed the dog as if her feet were a rarity more succulent than clams casino. In my thirties, as a young husband, I adopted a Gordon setter named Alex, a wise soul who stood watch over my wife and me right up until the day our first child was born. And then, as a father, I shared a house with Lucy, a retriever/chow chow mash-up who wasted exactly zero time in making clear her utter contempt—for me, for our children, for all of us. We'd come home each day to find the dog in a state of cynicism and disapproval. *Ohh,* she'd say, just like Tony Soprano's mother. *Look who calls.*

It was Lucy who was on duty the day I finally came down the stairs in heels. She looked me up and down with exhaustion. *Ugh,* she said. *I wish the Lord would take me now.*

Actually, a lot of people reacted like that at first, including many of the men and women I had loved most.

When we talk about dogs, it is not uncommon for people to say things like *They love us unconditionally! Their hearts are so pure!* But to be honest, I have rarely found this to be the case. When I was a boy, for instance, there was a German shepherd named Gomer who lived on a farm near our house. Most of his days were spent at the end of a heavy iron chain. If he'd been given the option, it was clear enough: Gomer would have torn me apart like a Walmart piñata. The only thing unconditional about Gomer's feelings toward me was his bottomless hate.

But his owner, Joy, saw in him an adorable rascal. *Who's a good boy?* she asked the terrible Gomer, feeding him a piece of raw steak she'd obtained specifically for this purpose. *Who's a good boy?*

In the years since, I have known lots of people whose love has been focused solely on other questionable creatures, some of them evil, such as Gomer, and others just sad and floppy, dogs with all the sentience of a used ShamWow. But oh, the adoration that my friends have had for these wuffly creatures, and with what profound devotion they've arranged their days around their needs. One friend of mine has a dog that is kind of like a miniature sloth, with unsettling bits of dried-up Alpo congealed into the fur around its mouth, a creature whose paws for reasons I do not understand can never touch the ground and who must be carried like a clutch purse from spot to spot. She calls him her "little man." She's always telling me about how much Bingo loves her, how Bingo's the only one who understands her, how her life would be empty were it not for the radiant adoration little Bingo sends forth.

I am not in the business of questioning the love that anyone has for anyone else, so let's agree: whatever she and Bingo have going on is their own sweet business.

But if you ask me, the magic of dogs is not that their love for us is unconditional. What's unconditional is the love that we have for *them*.

Listen: If we're going to talk about dogs, we're going to have to talk about love, and the sooner you get your mind around this, the more irritated with me you can be. I'll try to be brief.

I'm pretty sure that if there is any reason why we are here on this planet, it is in order to love one another. It is, as the saying goes, all ye know on earth, and all ye need to know.

And yet, as it turns out, nothing is harder than loving human beings.

In part, this is because we don't know what we want. Or, on those unlikely occasions when we *do* know what we want, we often don't know how to put our desire into words.

Instead, a lot of the time we act like my old friend Gomer, snarling and slathering at the end of our chains, driven to fury not only by our imprisonment but also by the presence of others who appear to us to be undeservedly walking free.

A lot of the time, the one thing we're here to do is the thing that we're actually not all that good at. When we try to express the thing we feel, most of the time it comes out wrong. *No, wait,* I have found myself saying over and over again, perhaps more than any other phrase I have uttered in this life. *That's not what I meant!*

On the other hand, given how inarticulate we are in the language of love, we're absolutely fluent when it comes to expressing our hate.

This is a book about dogs: the love we have for them and the way that love helps us understand the people we have been.

This is a book about men and boys, written by a woman who remembers the world in which they live the way an emigrant might, late in life, recall the distant country of her birth. Back when I lived in the Olde Country—like many men—there were times I found it impossible to express the thing that was in my heart. But the love I felt for dogs was one I never had cause to hide.

This is a book about seven phases of my life and the dogs I loved at each moment.

It's in the love of dogs, and my love for them, that I can best now take the measure of that vanished boy and his endless desire.

There are times when it is hard for me to fully remember that mysterious child, his ferocity—and his fragility. Sometimes he seems to fade before me, like breath on a mirror.

But I remember the dogs.

It's worth noting what happened on the one day Gomer finally got the thing he'd always wanted, by which I mean my throat.

Gomer's mistress, Joy, was the manager of a stable. There my sister rode horses and hung out with stable boys who mucked the stalls and listened to the Rolling Stones on a transistor radio. I was just a scarecrow in those days, hanging around the barn with my partner-in-crime, an older boy named Jimmy. That was my name, too, back then anyway, and we were like two mobsters: Jimmy Slingshot (him) and Jimmy Fly-trap (me). We shot wasps' nests with slingshots; we crept around the perimeter of the nearby Delaware County Prison and watched the convicts planting corn in their orange jumpsuits. We walked across farmers' fields with his dog, Fleece, who had only one eye. We sat in the leather seats of his brother's stock car, a coupe that sat up on blocks in the Slingshot family's garage. Its front fender was crushed, from an accident during the last race the brother had run.

The brother, Bob Junior, wasn't around anymore. Now he was in Vietnam, flying a chopper. While he was away, Jimmy Slingshot's father, Bob Senior—who had worked at Boeing developing the very chopper that his son was now flying—turned completely gray.

One day Jimmy Slingshot and I came upon a huge pile of dead pigs in a field. Flies swarmed around them.

What did we do? Just what you'd expect: we got out our slingshots and shot pebbles at the carcasses. That being the custom among our people.

I would, of course, have rather been back at our house, secretly experimenting with my mother's pink plastic rollers. But how could a person put this desire into words? The only thing you could do with such yearning—even if it was, ultimately, the utter truth of your being—was to keep it locked down in a hole. Or so I then thought.

In the afternoon I left his house and went looking for my sister, who was supposed to be currycombing her pony, Iris, down by the barn. In order to get there, though, I had to walk through Joy's farm, a place that had clearly once been a thriving enterprise but had fallen on some strange misfortune. The biggest of the old barns had burned down decades before, and it now stood collapsed in upon itself, a tangle of stone foundations and charred timbers. A series of old stone steps led from Jimmy Slingshot's house, down a hill, and into the heart of the old farm's ruins, a complex that included not only the barn with my sister's pony but Joy's home, too, a stone farmhouse surrounded by mud well pocked with hoofprints.

Gomer sat at his usual sentry post, the top step of Joy's front porch. A chain dangled from his neck.

I tried to slip by him without making eye contact—the dog hated nothing more than eye contact. But I heard the deep growl, and I froze, hoping against hope that motionlessness would make me less contemptible in his sight. In this I was wrong. Gomer leapt to his feet and barked at me with anger and contempt. Again and again he lunged, only to be yanked back by his chain. I felt my heart pounding. I was certain I knew why the dog hated me—it was because he could see into my heart. *I know who you are,* he snarled. *I know who you are!*

There were times when I figured everybody knew who I was— that I was not Jimmy Fly-trap at all, that I was, in fact, Jenny Twin-set. I really believed this, right up until the day I finally came out, some thirty years later. It wasn't that I held, and kept hidden, a nuclear secret that no one ever guessed. No, what I believed was the opposite: that everyone knew I was really a girl but was just too polite to say it.

All too polite, that is, except for creatures such as Gomer, creatures who measured their snarling self-worth in terms of truth telling. I'd recognize the shepherd's bark in the words of bullies many years later when they said things like *I'm sorry to hurt your feelings, but the most important thing is telling you the truth.* Which is, if you ask me, often another way of saying *The most important thing for me, in fact, is hurting your feelings, and doing so as deeply as I can.*

Gomer's chain snapped, and the dog unexpectedly found himself free.

No one was more surprised at this than Gomer, and the shepherd paused for a moment at the bottom of the wooden stairs, doubting his good fortune. The dog looked back at the house for a moment, as if he expected that the only possible consequence of finally getting free was someone coming along in that very same instant to chain him up again. In this, if only he'd known it, the dog and I turned out to have some common ground.

Instead, he turned toward me and lunged.

I was not fast on my feet, then or now, but I tried to outrun Gomer. I heard his furious snarling just behind me, along with what sounded like the *chomp* of the dog's teeth as they snapped through empty space. Finally his front paws struck me in the middle of the back, and I fell into the wet mud that surrounded Joy's farmhouse.

I lay on my stomach and closed my eyes, thinking the eleven-year-old equivalent of *Father, into Thy hands I commend my spirit.* The dog had his front paws on my spine. I felt his terrible breath on my neck. He barked triumphantly. *I got you, Jenny Twin-set,* he suggested. *I got you.*

And then, incredibly, I felt his tongue on my cheek.

Gomer sniffed me. Then he licked me again. The tongue was wet and rough.

A door slammed. Joy came out of the farmhouse. "What's going on out here?" she said with irritation, as if somehow, whatever this situation was, it was something I had brought upon myself, and—who knows?—maybe in this suspicion she was not wrong.

I heard her boots sucking through the mud, and then, as I rolled over, I saw her towering above me, reaching down for the links of Gomer's broken chain.

"Good boy," she said in a voice that seemed to contain both affection, and pity. "You're a good boy." For a moment I thought, *Wait, I am?* Then the inevitable conclusion ensued: *She means the dog.*

In the long years since then, I have often wondered what exactly about that boy was good. Surely it was not the terrorization of an eleven-year-old nerd that Joy was singling out for special praise. True, Joy was no fan of mine; she knew full well what Jimmy Slingshot and I were up to when we were out of her sight. Still, it couldn't have given her any pleasure—or not much, anyhow—to see me on the ground, literally afraid for my life.

No, what Joy must have felt for Gomer at that moment was gratitude for his protection. She was a woman who lived a hard life on a half-abandoned farm, and as difficult as it was for my young self to imagine, there were likely many moments when she felt vulnerable and scared. That frightening prison with its Victorian tower was less than a mile away, and now and again the word went out: a convict had gone over the wall. There were more than a few times that Jimmy Slingshot and I had been told to stay inside during a prison break, while police combed through the woods with bloodhounds and flashlights.

Sometimes I wondered who it was that had killed all those pigs

Jimmy Slingshot and I had found piled up in the field. Had it been an escaped prisoner, who'd done it simply out of malice and revenge?

Maybe, in addition to being a felon, he was a vegetarian.

You don't think of adults as being scared or vulnerable when you're a child, but the older you get, the more you understand that the world is a frightening place and that anyone standing between you and the universe's unseen terrors is someone for whom you can feel tremendous gratitude, even a kind of reverence. It did not matter that the person Gomer was protecting Joy from was a feline nerd who kept seahorses in a tank in his bedroom. What mattered was that even she sometimes felt alone and afraid and that in these moments Gomer made her heart feel less broken.

In his own slathering way, by knocking me to the ground, Gomer had demonstrated to Joy that something stood between her and danger. And by this action, as alone as she might have felt in the world, she knew she was not unloved.

One day in 2017, not long after Indigo died, I got a call from the place where we board our dogs when we're out of town, a "bed 'n' biscuit" called Willow Run. One of their customers was dying of cancer. Her dog, Chloe, was a black Lab, and she needed a home. We rolled our eyes.

They had to be kidding. We had been in mourning ever since we lost Indigo, and not just because the dog we had loved was gone but because the people we had been seemed to have vanished as well. We were just too banged up. We told them we were sorry, but no.

Then, one weekend when I picked up Ranger after an overnight at Willow Run, I met this Chloe. Her face was soft.

I asked, Maybe I could just take her home for a day? Well, you know how this story goes.

When Chloe entered our house, she was cautious and uncertain. She spent hours that first day going to every corner, sniffing things out. At the end of the day she sat down by the fireplace and gave me a look. *If you wanted,* she said, *I would stay with you.*

Soon enough, Ranger had a new wing-dog.

I had hopes of having a conversation with Chloe's owner before the end, trying to learn what their history had been. I wanted to bring Chloe over to her house so her owner could know that her dog had a good home and so that the two of them could have a proper farewell.

When I finally got through, though, I learned that Chloe's owner had died the week before.

It snowed that night, and I woke up in a room made mysterious by light and stillness. In the morning I sat up and found that Chloe had climbed into bed with us as we slept.

Well? she asked. I touched her soft ears in the bright, quiet room and thought about the gift of grace.

If you wanted, I said, *I would stay with you, too.*

Playboy, 1969

When I was young, Dad said,
people used to mess with me.

There we were, creeping around an abandoned racetrack, my friend Lloyd and me, looking for the grave. We didn't know the exact location. The departed was a Saint Bernard, though, so how hard could it be to find? We imagined a big mound of dirt, a headstone bearing the name TOBY. I held a bouquet of dandelions. In his hands Lloyd held nothing.

My parents were suspicious of Lloyd, who, being diabetic, often arrived at our house with syringes and insulin. We were only eleven years old, but the idea of needles in the house put my mother on edge. It was 1969, and Lloyd had long hair, and if there were needles in the house, heroin could not be far away, or so thought my mother, whose name, unexpectedly, was Hildegarde.

From down the long dirt road we heard the approach of a slow-moving car—tires on gravel. It was not yet twilight, but the car's headlights were on. They stabbed through the tall trees on either side of the access road, casting shadows.

"Hide," said Lloyd. I'd been thinking the same thing. We ran into the First Baptist Cemetery, which was just through the trees to our left. It hadn't occurred to us to look for Toby's grave there, what with the dog not being human. We hunkered down behind the stone for Elizabeth Wayne, who'd died in 1793. *She was a woman of distinguished piety and benevolence.* We knew that she'd been the mother of Revolutionary War hero "Mad" Anthony Wayne, who was interred over in the cemetery at the St. David's Friends meetinghouse, or most of him was, anyhow. We'd ridden our bikes there. After his death in 1796, the general had been buried up in Erie, but twelve years later Wayne's son Isaac had ridden his carriage to the grave site and dug his father up so he could be reinterred in St. David's. He dismembered the body by boiling it in a large kettle until he had only the bones. That being the fashion at the time.

These he drove back down to St. David's. The rest he left in Erie.

The car came up the drive and then paused by the cemetery. We heard the door open and close, then the footsteps drawing near. A flashlight played off of the headstones.

"Okay, boys," the voice said. "I think you can come out of there now."

Lloyd and I stood up. Dr. Boyer shone the light in our faces. She was the veterinarian. Her practice was in the farmhouse at the end of the road, on the edge of the abandoned racetrack. There was a windmill by her farmhouse. Its sails were broken.

"Lloyd Goodyear," she said in a voice that implied, *I might have known.* "And Jimmy Boylan."

"Yes, ma'am," I said.

"Paying your respects?" she said, shining her light on the dandelions in my hand.

"We're looking for Toby," said Lloyd.

Dr. Boyer was a ruddy-faced woman with short hair and freckles. "Your dog," she said.

"Yes, ma'am," I said. She knew all about Toby. It was to Dr. Boyer's practice that Lloyd's mother, Breda, had taken the dog's body, after Lloyd had seen it on the median strip on his way to Marple Newtown Junior High that autumn. The dog had been missing for a week by then.

"We heard he was buried out here," said Lloyd. "We wanted to see it."

Dr. Boyer stood there, considering us.

"That's the worst story I've ever heard," she said.

Lloyd and I both opened our mouths to respond, because clearly a response was called for. But what could we say? We'd had plenty of experience lying to adults, and it was not uncommon to get caught. In those situations, the only thing you could do was tell the truth and take your licks. Sometimes you could try to explain why the circumstances had demanded mendacity—especially if the situation had called for protecting certain people from the world's cruelties.

The truth had always been my last recourse. You knew that when you came out with the truth, no matter how humiliating its revelation might be, you couldn't be punished for it. Or at least that had been my understanding. Now, for the first time in my life, I experienced what it was like to tell someone the truth and not to be believed.

As it turned out, there were times when the truth was no help at all.

"We heard—," I started, but Lloyd was already looking down at the ground. He knew that it was pointless trying to explain. "We heard that he was buried here."

"In the *Baptist cemetery*?" Dr. Boyer said. "The dog?"

"No, ma'am," I said. "On the farm."

Now I was just pissing her off. "But who," she asked incredulously, "who would bury a dog—*here*?"

The obvious answer, and the one we had believed to be true, of course, was, *Why, you, Dr. Boyer*. But this could not be spoken. Instead, I joined my friend in the universal pose of humiliation and stared down at the ground with him. There we stood, two shamefaced boys.

"You boys get off this property," said Dr. Boyer. "I don't ever want to see you here again. Do you understand?"

"Yes, ma'am," I said.

"Go on," said the doctor. "Get."

We turned and walked out of the cemetery, through the cluster of dead Waynes. From behind us came the sound of her car door opening and closing and the tires scraping on the dirt and the gravel.

"She didn't believe us!" I said to Lloyd, furious.

But Lloyd didn't answer back. I looked over at him to see fat tears rolling down his face. I didn't say anything about it, because we were boys, and our code was clear: the only way to respond to some of the most important things in our world was with silence.

By the time I got home, Dr. Boyer had already called my parents. My mother told me to go into the den. "Your father wants to talk to you," she said in a voice without pity.

Dick Boylan—a handsome man with a crisp white shirt, a thin tie, and slicked-back hair—sat in a black leather chair smoking an L&M King. Our dalmatian dog, Playboy, lay on the floor, his legs pointing into the air, displaying his pink belly and his not inconsiderable nether dog parts.

"Had a little run-in with Dr. Boyer?" said my father in a tone that was both sympathetic and disappointed.

"We were looking for Toby's grave," I explained, although why my father should believe this when it had failed with the woman we'd been told had *actually buried the dog* there I don't know.

"Sit down," he said, and I collapsed on the couch. The den was a small room off of the living room. There was a black-and-white TV in one corner and three walls of books. During the weekend, Lloyd and I sometimes glued together models of battleships here.

"We really were looking for it," I said.

My father took a drag on his cigarette and held the smoke in his lungs for a very long time. Then he blew it out. He took off his tortoiseshell glasses, wiped them with a pocket handkerchief.

"Lloyd's a good guy," my father said thoughtfully. He put his glasses back on. "You're very loyal to him."

"He's my friend," I said.

"He's got some challenges that you don't have," said my father.

"The diabetes," I said.

"No," said my father. "I wasn't thinking about that per se."

Playboy's tail thumped against the hooked rug. I noticed that, at this inopportune moment, the dog's private regions were beginning to pulse. A pink suggestion began to poke at the outer boundaries of its sheath.

"You weren't?"

My father took another long drag on his cigarette.

"You know," he said, "my father died when I was just about your age. When I was twelve."

There was an oil painting of my grandfather that hung in our living room. I had nightmares about it fairly regularly. In my dreams, the old man was trying to get out of the painting. He wanted to get me.

"It can upend a young man," my father said, "if he doesn't have . . . determination."

Lloyd's father had died of a heart attack the summer before. We'd been shooting off model rockets on the playground one afternoon. I remember the strange feeling of being on the school grounds in summer, when the place was as abandoned as Dr. Boyer's farm. I had a two-stage rocket called the Black Widow. We watched as it took off in the sky and disappeared. The parachute had malfunctioned. That night, Lloyd called me on the phone and said, "My dad had a heart attack. They took him to the hospital, but they couldn't help him. So he died."

I did not know what to tell my friend.

"Is that what you think he needs?" I said to my father, uncertain. "Determination?"

"I think," he said, "it is the thing you need."

I sat there, taking this all in. I wasn't sure exactly what it was we were talking about. It was not entirely impossible that my father suspected what lurked in my heart and was suggesting that it might be resisted, if only I approached the question of being alive with the necessary resolve and firmness.

On the floor, Playboy's exuberance burst forth. A lack of determination wasn't one of his problems, that much was certain.

The following year I entered a new school, Haverford, which was for boys only. Lloyd, for his part, followed the rest of my classmates to Marple Newtown. I cried and cried in my parents' bedroom the night before I started at Haverford, saying, *Please don't make me go. I'll miss my friends.*

This was not the real reason I did not want to go to an all-boys school, of course, but the real reason was not one that I could speak out loud. I could barely even whisper it to myself, because who could want the thing that I wanted? How could such a fate be granted? It was stupid to even think about.

But I thought about it.

On my first day at the new school, my father dropped me off at the gates on his way to the train station in Haverford. Unfortunately, my father was catching a 7:00 A.M. train into Philly, and school did not begin until 8:30. That left me alone on the campus wearing a coat and tie. There was no one else around.

The door to the middle school was open, though, and I knew my way around from having attended summer school there in the summer of 1970. I'd sat in the huge study hall doing hundreds of math problems, one after the other, as sweat trickled down the sides of my face. There were shades on the windows that were raised or lowered by small ropes. Each one was tied in a noose.

In that study hall I'd sat next to a young man named Zero. Eighteen years later, he would be the best man at my wedding. But I didn't know that then.

Now I walked through the middle school. None of the lights were on. I made my way to my homeroom, where the master's name was written on the board in chalk: MR. PARSONS. There was a diagram of the desks in the room and our last names written in each one. I found the desk indicated by the name BOYLAN.

In Irish, Boylan means "Oath Breaker." Or, to put it more succinctly, "Liar." It's a good name for a literary memoirist, actually. In

Irish you spell my name O Baoigheallain. My people had been kings in County Monaghan in the twelfth century but had been wiped out by the McMahons, the bastards. Now I, the descendant of kings, walked through a deserted junior high with a little briefcase.

I sat there at my desk in the empty classroom in the empty building and looked at my watch. It was 7:15 A.M. On the board was also written the titles of the books we would be reading during the coming term: *The Yearling. Prester John. The Story of a Bad Boy. The Moonstone. Johnny Tremain.*

After a while I got up and wandered around the rest of the middle school building. I went downstairs to find my locker, which was located in a dark, cement room. I couldn't find the light switch. I wandered down a long corridor of ancient lockers until I found mine. There was nothing inside.

Lloyd Goodyear and the other boys and girls I'd known since kindergarten were now starting their semester at Marple Newtown Junior High. Back in elementary school, I'd been the class clown, a regular Don Rickles. Because I did well in school, this was generally tolerated. But in my sixth-grade year, everything went south. "You are struggling," said my father. "You never struggled before."

One day at school all the girls had been taken off to a special assembly. The boys weren't allowed in. When they came back to join us, they seemed angry.

"What's bothering you?" my father had asked me. I didn't know what to tell him.

The door to the locker room opened and closed, and I heard someone enter the dark space. There was also the sound of something heavy dragging against the floor. For reasons I cannot explain, I made the decision not to let this stranger know I was there. It was easy enough to hide at the end of the long row of rusted green lockers in the lightless space. Now there was a noise like *plap*, followed by a wet dragging sound. Then another *plap*.

A human voice hummed softly to itself, slightly off tune. *Plap.* "I've got peace like a river, I've got peace like a river, in my soul." *Plap.*

The voice sounded as if it belonged to a very old man. There was something gurgling in his throat as he sang. I saw a shadow play against the far wall. I could tell that he was moving away from where I lay hidden. Slowly I edged down the line of old lockers. The door was not far.

I reached out for the handle. Something went *plap.* Water sprayed onto my gray flannel trousers and I turned.

There stood a black man about sixty. His face was completely distorted by some sort of growth or cyst. It bloomed from the side of his face like a head of broccoli. In one hand he held a mop.

The man and I looked at each other and screamed.

I pushed through the door out into the hallway and ran toward the stairs. When I reached the top I paused, out of breath. I looked back. I was not being pursued.

I made my way back to Mr. Parsons's homeroom and sat there at my desk. I opened up my backpack and got out the book we would be reading, *The Story of a Bad Boy*, by Thomas Bailey Aldrich. *This is the story of a bad boy, it began. Well, not such a very bad, but a pretty bad boy; and I ought to know, for I am, or rather I was, that boy myself. . . .*

But let us begin at the beginning.

My father's father had died in 1940, when my dad was only twelve and my grandfather fifty-two. *His* father, my great-grandfather, had died at age fifty. All the Boylan sons had lost their fathers early.

Just as I would lose my own father in a few years, just as my own sons, decades later, would lose theirs, although in a slightly different manner.

I had been enrolled that fall in a weekend course in which I assembled a gasoline-powered model airplane in an elementary school classroom. On Saturday mornings I was dropped off at the school in Springfield, the next town over, and in I went, walking down the hallways of a school where I knew no one. Along with my fellow inmates I glued a frame together from a balsa kit, then stretched silk over the frame, coated the silk with dope, fitted in the propeller, laid in the delicate ailerons. We were assigned desks and used the same ones each weekend. But of course these desks were the property of other students who spent the week there, people whom I would never know. I was given the desk of a girl whose name was Denise. Her name was written out on a large piece of lined paper that was affixed to the front of the desk. She kept a pair of barrettes in her desk, along with her other stuff—a plastic bag of mini Kleenex, her crayons, all of her schoolbooks. I sanded the elements of my balsa-wood plane surrounded by these traces of the life of some invisible girl.

My mother had enrolled me in the airplane-glue colloquium because she was worried about me, and not without good reason. It was her theory that getting me out of the house might make me more like the sons of her friends. They played sports, these boys, joined Little League, had friends. Unlike me, they didn't build *Gemini* capsules in the corner of their room and explore imaginary planets with a dalmatian as copilot. They did not spend long hours inside of a box marked ROBOTRON 9000. To be sure, I was extremely entertaining, in short bursts, but my only real interest outside of the space program was carnivorous plants. I kept a broken aquarium full of Venus flytraps in my room, which I fed roast beef and scrapple. I'd had the seahorses, too, but they all died.

One weekend, slightly stoned on airplane dope, I reached into Denise's desk. I held her little plastic yellow barrettes in my fingers. I looked around the room. All around me were boys wacked out on glue, making progress. My hands fell upon Denise's crayons.

Slowly, my hands completely out of sight, I removed the crayons from the box. With malice aforethought, I snapped each one in half. I couldn't see them, but I imagined them in her desk, the red and purple and the burnt umber, each one ruined. I sat there stunned by the thing I had done and pictured this Denise coming into school and finding her crayons broken, her eyes filling with tears at the random injustice of the world. I wasn't sorry.

"All right, Playboy," I said to the dalmatian. "It's time for you and me to get into the box."

The dog knew what that meant.

My father had done his best. He'd bought me a baseball glove, which I tended with neat's-foot oil and placed beneath my pillow as I slept. I liked the way the glove smelled, with its promise of summer. But I was more interested in smelling the glove than in catching any actual baseballs with it.

The box was in the basement. A few months earlier, it had contained a new refrigerator. Now it was decorated with a Magic Marker, with drawings of magnetic tape reels and blinking lights. A sign bore the legend ROBOTRON 9000 THE ANSER MACHINE.

The dog and I climbed into the box, booted up the system.

My parents and sister entered the house. Next to the Anser Machine was an inflatable punching clown. "Boing," I suggested.

"Ugh," said my sister, and stormed right through the basement and up the back stairs. You couldn't blame her. She had friends with brothers the same age as me, and instead of spending the day inside of Robotron 9000 with the dog, *they* played songs on guitar about ending the war.

"Jimmy," my mother said, "come out of the box."

Boing, I replied.

"I'll write down some questions," my father told her, as if to say, *I'll handle this.*

There was a long pause. I looked down at my feet at Playboy. He growled resentfully, to let me know—as if I didn't already—that this whole enterprise was doomed.

I heard my father writing upon an index card with the pencil I had thoughtfully attached to a string on the front of the Anser Machine. After a moment, the card came through the slot.

What can you hold without touching? he asked.

The dog looked up at me. *Well, Robotron?* Playboy observed. *He's got you there.*

Even though we no longer went to the same school, I would occasionally spend a weekend at Lloyd Goodyear's house. It was pretty clear our paths were diverging, though. One Saturday I arrived at his house to find two girls lying around Lloyd's room. They were listening to Mott the Hoople.

Lloyd was lying on the bed with one of the girls. The other lay on the floor next to the record player. She looked me up and down, then said to Lloyd, "This is your friend?"

Later we all wound up on the playground of our old school, Culbertson Elementary. Lloyd and his girl climbed the backstop of the baseball diamond and sat there suspended high above home plate, going to first base. The other girl and I sat on a bench in the dugout. Something about the situation suggested that if Lloyd got into a jam, either she or I would be summoned by the coach to warm up in the bullpen.

But Lloyd found himself in no jam. By all appearances, he was on his way to pitching a perfect game.

I didn't know what to say to this girl or how to say it. I think in my heart I wanted to say something like *What is it like being you?*

But it wasn't the kind of question you could ask, and even if you did, how would she respond? In my experience, it turns out that many people don't have the slightest clue what it would be like not to be themselves and, in fact, find the question kind of strange. But of course, it was all I could think about.

On the field before us, not so long ago, we had shot off model rockets that had disappeared in the blue skies of Pennsylvania. Off to the right was a flowering laurel tree. One recess, Lloyd and I had sat beneath its branches and eaten the flowers. We missed the call back to class, and the teacher, Miss Wolff, had remarked upon our empty chairs. *They're eating flowers,* she was told. When we finally got back to the class, Miss Wolff just looked at us as if she knew something about us we did not.

From over our heads came the sound of laughter.

I turned to the girl I was with and said, *You know, we could get us a couple of malteds.* I did not know what malteds were, but I knew that getting us a couple of them was what you were supposed to do, if you wanted to be in love.

For years we'd just let Playboy run free, which suited his resentful, mulish character just fine. It suited Sawmill Road as well, a place that was an even mix of Christopher Robin's enchanted Hundred Acre Wood and that forest where they filmed *The Blair Witch Project.*

The village—Newtown Square, Pennsylvania—had been settled in the eighteenth century by Quakers from Wales. There were three Quaker meetinghouses and a shuttered one-room octagonal schoolhouse. Miles and miles of the township were made up of dense forest. There were farms, too—rolling hills dotted with Angus cows and horses. One of our neighbors was Mrs. du Pont, on Liseter Farm. Years later, her son would murder a wrestling coach on their property. They made a movie out of the tragedy: *Foxcatcher.* Steve Carell was in it. He wasn't usually given to fake noses, but he made an exception in this instance.

Our road cut through a swath of the old forest. On one side of Sawmill were a dozen late-1950s split-level homes. On the other was the forbidding and beautiful expanse of Earle's Woods, ten square miles of hardwood jungle originally owned by George Earle—who'd been governor back in the late 1930s and whose fancy country estate stood on the banks of a lake in the heart of the forest. A half dozen other houses had been built in those woods as well. But something had happened, I don't know what. Earle's mansion stood half burned and partially tumbled in upon itself. An overgrown cobblestone road led from the ruined house in the woods to the others, which were also fallen in, wrecked. Some of the abandoned houses looked almost inhabitable and still had curtains in the windows.

Years later, I would have a conversation with Governor Earle's daughter. She said that the houses in the woods had once belonged to the people who worked in her father's mansion. She'd been to the estate only once—in the mid-1960s, when she and a bunch of her teenage friends drank beer on the banks of Earle's Lake. Mid-revel, some cops had scooped the young people up, and the police chief made a phone call to the ex-governor, asked him how his daughter and her friends might be treated.

Send them to jail, said he.

During the Revolutionary War, those woods had been haunted by a legendary figure named James Fitzpatrick, whom the locals called Sandy Flash. Once, in disguise, he'd attended a meeting in the one-room schoolhouse where plans were made to arrest him. After pulling the sergeant aside, he revealed his identity, tied him up, and robbed him. *You wanted to see Captain Fitz, sir, and now you have seen him,* he said. Sometimes he dressed himself up like a scarecrow and rode through the woods on his horse, cackling. He lingered in this place. I'd lain awake in my bed on summer nights and heard the sound of horses' hooves softly clopping on the cobblestones in the forest.

We'd started keeping Playboy on a leash. Before that, we'd just open the door and let him roam. He'd head into Earle's Woods, disappear for hours. Sometimes he'd come back with his belly engorged and a strangely smug expression on his face. It wasn't clear what he'd been eating, but it wasn't dog food.

Motorcycles drove the dog insane. We'd hear the Harleys coming down Sawmill long before we'd see them, and if Playboy was close enough, we'd grab him by the choke chain and try to restrain him. Sometimes he gave us the slip anyhow. Then he bounded toward the passing motorcyclist and attempted to bite the legs of the rider. No one ever fell off his hawg as a result of Playboy's attack, but it was not unusual to see the cyclists wobbling back and forth in an attempt to escape our terrible dog. Over the roar of the Shovelheads we could hear the screaming and the swearing. One day Playboy got hold of someone's pant leg and was dragged down the road for a hundred feet or so until at last the denim ripped. Playboy stood in the middle of Sawmill Road watching as the motorcycle receded, jeans cuff in his mouth. The driver raised high one hand, middle finger extended, as he soared around the far curve that led up toward the Biddles' farm-house and the old racetrack for sulkies and carriage drivers beyond that.

Over thirty years later, as I was riding toward home with my friend Tim, after the surgery I had been dreaming of for most of my life, he asked me for the name of my first dog and the name of the street where I had been a child. "This," Tim said, "is how you generate your porn star name."

I told him that, following this rule, my porn name would be Play-boy Sawmill.

In response, Tim began to laugh so hard that for a long time he could not speak but could only clutch his abdomen as if afraid he might explode.

Back in the 1960s, though, the members of my family were humil-iated by owning such a terrible dog. The exception being my father, who was incapable of finding fault with the dalmatian, no matter how heinous his behavior. My father liked to sit in a leather chair in our den, smoking his L&M Kings and watching the black-and-white television, the dog's front paws in his lap. Dick Boylan had short hair oiled back with Vitalis, and tortoiseshell spectacles that made him look a little like the history professor he'd always wanted to become. (Instead of being a trust banker at Philadelphia's Provident National, which was what he wound up as instead after my grandmother "drank the money.") On Sunday nights Dick made Jiffy Pop for his family and then we gathered around the set to watch *Walt Disney's Wonderful World of Color* in black-and-white. My mother brought in a glass pitcher filled with ice water. My uncle Al had given it to her as a wedding present, but we didn't know where he was now. Uncle Al rode around the country on boxcars. When he was on the East Coast, he stayed with my aunt Erna and her husband, Jack, who was a rail-road detective. They lived above a train station in Glen Mills. All day long, the freights went by and shook the house. My Prussian grand-mother lived there, too, but she wouldn't get out of bed without her teeth. No one knew where the teeth were.

"Who's a good boy?" my father asked, scratching the terrible Play-boy behind his ears. On the television, a black-and-white kaleidoscope pulsed and flowered as sweet voices sang the show's theme song. My father rubbed Playboy's thick neck, and the dog's back leg thumped up and down in ecstasy. "Who's a good boy?"

All through my childhood, from my earliest memory right up to the day Lloyd and I sought in vain for the grave of Toby, a voice whis-pered in my heart: *You are not you.*

I suspect, in fact, that this is a nearly universal human complaint. And yet, if a haunted, harrowing sense of inauthenticity is common-place, feeling that gender is the source of that inauthenticity is proba-bly more of a rarity. If you've never experienced a sense of dysphoria with your own body, all I can say is, *Lucky you.* But just because you have not experienced this yourself does not mean it is not real in the hearts of others.

How one reacts to that sense of wrongness is a mixture of char-acter, and circumstance, and the randomness of privilege. In my own case, in spite of how weird I felt inside, the only strategy for survival I could come up with was, *I guess I'll just try to make the best of things.* Because back then I could not imagine how a person might change.

After sixty years, my life falls into three eras: boyhood, manhood, and womanhood—each lasting about twenty years, plus or minus. I know that people like to publish angry "think pieces" calling the hu-manity of people like me into question, but please. How shall I refute such people? I shall refute them by living.

But, that said, it has to be admitted that my womanhood is different from that of most other women if only because I arrived here after forty years walking around undercover and after having internalized so much of the privilege that that subterfuge provided. True—it wasn't privilege I especially wanted; every day felt like Halloween. But that experience is different from that of most of the other women I know.

The difference between other women and me is really not about internal organs—after all, my aunt Erna never had a functioning uterus, and no one ever wrote an angry op-ed in *The New York Times* accusing *her* of not being who she thought she was. Nor is it chromosomes—and not only because there are plenty of women who suffer from something called "androgen insensitivity syndrome," women who may have a Y chromosome and *never even know it*. You can think of an exception for pretty much any gender marker you can come up with, from men who are unafraid to ask for directions to women who really, *really* like the Three Stooges.

What makes me different from other women at this late hour is neither chromosomes nor ovaries nor the fact that I can play "A Whiter Shade of Pale" on a Hammond organ. What makes me different, in the end, is history.

Sometimes I think of myself as a gender emigrant, someone born in a different country—dear old BoyLand. When I had enough agency to undertake the voyage, I made a difficult ocean crossing and washed up on the shores of GirlLand, where I have dwelled happily for the last twenty years. I have my green card here in the country of women, and I have a patriotism for this place that is unique, perhaps, to people who began life somewhere else. And yet I do have a trace of a foreign accent about me, stray behaviors and tempers that ring with the far-off music of the Olde Country.

I do not know what people see when they look at me now, but I suspect offhand that they do not see a fabulous knockout; what they see, if anything, is a tired-looking older woman with high-tech hearing aids. People who don't know me often guess, upon meeting me, that I'm a teacher of some kind or a minister. When they learn my history, they don't throw up their hands in amazement and shout, *No! No! But you're so gorgeous! It can't be!*

Usually people nod kindly at me and say something that reflects their utter lack of surprise, like *Is that the fact.*

It used to be that this hurt my feelings. I wanted to be beautiful, and I wanted to be thin, and I wanted my appearance—my ability to *slay*—to argue for the fact of my womanhood. I wanted my outsides to provide the most persuasive rhetorical case for my insides.

Now, I don't care quite so much, and not only because I know my heart makes a better case for my identity than a little button nose. It's also because my womanhood can't be taken away from me anymore—not by the heartless, not by someone's clever gender theory, not even by the mirror. After sixty years, time has caught up with me, even though when I first popped out of the box, I spent several years as a little cupcake. Oh, what fun that was while it lasted.

The question that remains for me, though, is: What does it *mean* to be a woman who had a boyhood? Is boyhood even the right word for it? How were the lessons of masculinity taught to me, and what aspects of those lessons still remain in my heart, all these many years later?

We had cats back in the day, including one my sister named *Baboing!*, which one morning was run over by a school bus that I then had to climb aboard. My mother, standing in the veterinarian's office later, was asked what the cat's name was, and there, with the dead thing in her arms, my dignified, sorrowful mother had to speak the words of truth:

"Ba-boing!" said she.

But I have been drawn to dogs above all, perhaps because my own personality is fundamentally canine. I am happiest when I am with those whom I love, preferably by a warm fire. If you lost something, I would try to bring it back to you.

If you and I were ever to part, I would be grief-stricken. If we were to meet again, I would be overjoyed and stunned—I never thought I'd see you again! I can't believe you're back! This is fantastic!

The saddest moment of any day is the moment my wife turns her light off on her side of the bed, and I feel crushed: *The day is over! There is no more fun to be had. It's all finished!*

This is when Deirdre just smiles and says, *We'll do more things together tomorrow, Jenny. There are many more days for us ahead.*

I lay my head down on my pillow, unconvinced. I never want this life to be over. I want to live forever and spend each day making sure you understand the depth of the love I have for you. I sleep with one eye open, just in case anything comes creeping for us as we dream. Even now I can hear Sandy Flash's laughter, echoing through the summer night.

You wanted to see Ba-boing!, *sir, and now you have seen him.*

October 1, 1970, was a Thursday. It was unusual for us to do anything on a school night, but my father felt that the occasion called for the unusual. And so Lloyd Goodyear and my father and I went in to Philadelphia to see the final game played in Connie Mack Stadium, Phillies versus Expos.

The park had been there, on the corner of 21st Street and Lehigh, for over sixty years. It had originally been built for the Philadelphia Athletics, but the Phillies moved in after the A's decamped for Kansas

City in 1955. It was an old-school ballpark with wooden seats and a strange corner tower that looked as if it would have been more at home on the roof of the Addams Family mansion. Now it was a rat-trap with a losing team in a bad neighborhood. By the next year, the Phils would move over to the new Veterans Stadium in South Philly.

My father and I had gone to many games there over the years, back in the days when the star Phillie was one Jim Bunning, a man who many years later would be described by *Time* magazine as one of the country's five worst senators and quite possibly mentally ill. He was no longer in a Phillies uniform by the time my father and Lloyd Goodyear and I showed up in 1970, though, to watch as the Phils beat the Expos in ten innings, and all around us, fans tore apart the stadium. Well before the ninth inning the place was echoing with the sounds of sawing and hammering, boards snapping, men yelling. It was more than a little bit frightening, and I remember my father looking around us, a hot dog in one hand, with an expression that made it clear he wondered if coming to see the last game in the old stadium was a good idea. I was frightened by the violence, afraid that before the game was over, we'd be thirty thousand people sitting in a giant pile of splintered wood.

But my friend Lloyd just looked around at the melee with delight. I think he was undaunted by the prospect of trouble. It had been a long time since he'd felt safe in the first place.

Lloyd got up at one point to go to the men's room and inject himself with insulin. My father and I sat there watching the game, watching the men in front of us taking a crowbar to their entire row of seats. How did they get into the park with a crowbar in the first place? As their seat splintered free from the floor, they cheered. My father looked over at me. "We're here for history," he said.

Lloyd came back after a long absence. "You okay?" I asked. He nodded.

The Phils finally prevailed in the tenth inning. After the victory, fans poured onto the field as others snapped the slats out of the seats in which they had been sitting. "Mr. Boylan," Lloyd asked, his eyes wide, "can we go down on the field?"

It had never occurred to me that we would want to join in the fracas. My father, fortunately, shook his head and ushered us out into the streets in search of our car. Everywhere you looked there were people carrying pieces of wood.

We got in the Ford Falcon and headed back toward Newtown Square. Lloyd looked out the window as we drove down Broad Street. "That was the greatest baseball game I ever saw," he said.

On our way to Lloyd's house we passed the cemetery where his father was buried. It was late at night by now, and long shadows played over the graves. No one spoke a word.

Sometimes, when I think back on the world of men, it's this night that comes first to mind. All that jubilant destruction, and in its wake, our silence. It was a world in which the most important things could rarely be spoken out loud, and had to be inferred, instead, through the alternating tongues of raucous, boneheaded stunts (on the one hand) or eloquent, painful silence (on the other).

I cannot ever remember my father saying, "I love you," although I never doubted the fullness of his heart. Once, when he was trying to show me how to use a soldering iron (I had broken a toy flying saucer), he accidentally scorched one of my fingers with the iron, and I cried out in pain. My father dropped everything and clutched me to his chest. "I'm so sorry," he said, his voice trembling. "My boy. I'm so sorry. I just want you to be all right."

If my father, like many men, was reluctant to spill his goobers, he had no such reservations when it came to Playboy, whom he fed chicken from the table, with whom he got down on the floor and wrestled.

Maybe my father, like a lot of men, was able to express for dogs what he could not say to people.

It wasn't just Playboy Dick Boylan was adoring when he rolled that dog upon his back and scratched his belly until the dalmatian's back leg thumped against the floor. It was all of us—his children, his wife, and the ridiculous, glorious life we shared. Maybe that's what he was trying to tell us, as he carved a drumstick from the chicken and gave it directly to Playboy. *I am playing with this terrible dog because I love you.*

We'd gotten Playboy from a kennel called Whispering Winds. We weren't his first owners. Someone had taken the puppy home, had him around for a year or so, then thought better of it. Who were these people? What name did they give him?

Whoever they were, they hadn't succeeded with the house-training. Playboy wasn't above squatting down in the living room and leaving—as the Irish song might have it—*a token he'd been there-o.* My father thought this was kind of funny, but then he was never the person who had to clean it up.

That task fell to my mother, a woman who never quite felt that this was her natural calling. She'd arrived in the country in 1923 via Ellis Island, and she and her six siblings settled along with their mother in what she later referred to as a "dirt farm" in Williamstown, New Jersey. One day, she came back from church and asked her mother why the pastor, in reading the Twenty-third Psalm, said *his head was running over.* The German word for head being *Kopf.* My grandfather appeared and disappeared. The youngest boy, Wilhelm, died in infancy. The oldest daughter, Gertrude, became a seamstress, and the older of the two sons, Roland, dropped out after seventh grade and became a milkman. My mother read books and played the banjo and worked at a soda fountain. One day, when she was in high school, a wild-eyed hobo came into the store, looked at her, and announced, *"Ich bin dein Vater."*

The next morning, she found him drunk in the pigpen. She had to get Roland to help her haul their father out of the sty. He took off after he woke up, and they didn't see the man again for a couple of decades, when he turned up at the New York City morgue. The only way they'd recognized him was that he was missing the end of the third finger on one hand. He'd lost this back in the 1930s, when he worked in an auto-body plant.

Hildegarde and Gertrude told New York they didn't want him. So he was buried on Hart Island, the potter's field of the city. I did a story on Hart Island when I was in my twenties, working for a magazine, not knowing at the time that my grandfather's bones were right there at my feet. In graduate school I wrote a short story about Hart Island, something about a boy who loses his father and a chimpanzee that rides a unicycle.

My mother eventually got away from the dirt farm and started working for book publishers in New York and Philadelphia. She swore that she'd never get married, having seen the ruin that her own mother's love for her feckless husband had brought about, and she kept that pledge until just shy of her fortieth birthday, when she was taking an accounting course being taught by a droll young Irishman, my father, who was twelve years her junior. She'd been a successful career woman for almost twenty years, having left the world of pigs and men behind. But then she fell.

Everyone was happy about the marriage, except my father's mother, Gammie, who had hoped for something more along the lines of Audrey Hepburn. Toward the end of her life, begrudgingly accepting the fact of my mother's goodness, Gammie told her, "Well, I guess it could have been worse. You could have been some *hussy.*"

And so my mother had given it all up—her lunches with Bennett Cerf, the autograph parties for celebrity authors, her train trips to publishing conventions in Chicago. All of this she left behind and became the mother of two—Cyndy when she was forty, me when she was forty-one. She liked being a mother. After all those years of being part of a family that was defined by poverty and absence, it was as if she got a chance to get things right.

And then came Playboy. She'd turned fifty years old right around the time he first burst through our doors, and there he was, a resentful, dangerous creature who gave nary a fuck about her earlier success in the publishing industry. Was she reminded, as she bent down to clean the rug with a roll of paper towels and a bucket of Mr. Clean, of her days as a child yanking her drunken father out of the pigpen?

"This creature has to go," she said to my father after Playboy had left another steaming pyramid beneath the baby grand piano. "I'm not here to clean up dog dirt!"

My father loved my mother with all his heart. But he was partial to Playboy. "Honey," he explained, "he's just a dog."

"I know what he is," my mother snapped.

Zero was one of my first friends at the new school, and we were almost surely drawn together because we were both outliers. The first time he came to my house he was driven by his mother in a red Cadillac convertible. Playboy burst out of the house and put his paws up on the side of the car, in which Zero and his mother now sat, terrified.

I came outside and yanked Playboy away from my new friend's neck. His mother gave him a concerned look and then drove off in the Caddy.

Zero looked at me, a little worried. Playboy snarled at him.

"Does your dog bite?" he asked.

I thought about it. "Yeah," I said. "Pretty much."

Two other friends, John and Link, also stayed overnight at my house that night, after having been dropped off by their own mothers. Playboy didn't try to kill them, though, maybe because each of them owned dogs of their own (unlike Zero) and already knew better than to take Playboy's huffing and puffing too seriously. John had a beagle named Snuffy. Link had a sad, lumpy dog named Moogus. Link had named her after the lady in the poem with the rings on her fingers and bells on her toes.

For she will have Moogus wherever she goes.

We all stayed overnight in the rec room. Once it had been my aunt Gertrude's living room, back when she lived with us. It had seemed like just a few years earlier when my adorable, eccentric aunt lived in an attic bedroom, listening to big-band records. On the very floors where now we slept, my aunt had once practiced the tango.

In the morning my sister walked through the rec room en route to a horse show, wearing boots and jodhpurs and a hard hat and a frilly shirt and carrying a whip. "Good morning, boys," she said.

A couple of weeks ago, I asked Link if he remembered this.

"Of course I remember that, my first glimpse of your sister," said he. "I've never forgotten it. That whip! The boots!" He sighed. "It's haunted me for fifty years. It wrecked me for everything else, forever."

She made an impression.

At Marple Newtown, Lloyd wore love beads and hung out with long-haired boys who exuded a mixture of irony and contempt. I owned no love beads. Instead, I glued together models of the human heart, the eye, a nose. In a terrarium in my room I grew my crop of insectivorous plants, including the Venus flytraps that I fed with crickets and ground beef. The Venus flytraps lived in a kind of peaty swamp. Since the glass in the terrarium was broken, this substance leaked very, very slowly through the cracks and fell onto the floor, where Playboy would lap it up with his pink and spotted tongue.

Lloyd did have one otherworldly talent. He was a near virtuoso on the cello, and on those weekends when he came to stay the night at our house, he would sit in a chair in our living room, his cello clasped between his legs, and he would close his eyes and draw his bow across the strings. My father and Playboy would come in and listen to him play the Bach Cello Suite no. 1 in G Major. We sat there, the three of us plus the dog, listening to the music.

There was something incredibly sad about Lloyd's expression as he played the cello.

At the time, I just thought the music made him sad. But now, of course, I think about Lloyd's father, whom he lost, and then Toby the St. Bernard, whom he'd lost as well. Had it really been his dog we'd been looking for, in fact, that day he and I went skulking around Dr. Boyer's farm?

Just as my father did not quite have a language for his love, my friend did not quite have a language for his loss. All that grief had to stay locked inside, in the world of boys and men.

He had the cello, though.

My grandfather, from his portrait upon the wall, scowled down at all of us. According to Gammie, Grampa had owned a dog once, too—Blackie was its name. A Scottie.

Many years later, after my family had moved from Newtown Square, I found myself driving through town around sunset. I didn't get back there that often. I think I was in college by then.

A music store with a big lit-up quarter note stood right off of a traffic roundabout. It was there that I saw Lloyd Goodyear, probably twenty years old by now. He had hair down to his belt buckle. Lloyd leaned against a wall, smoking a cigarette. He was alone. Next to him on the wall, in spray paint, were the words U.S. OUT OF NORTH AMERICA!

I thought of pulling over, telling him who I was, but instead I kept driving. I didn't know what I could tell him.

In my fifties, someone from our grade school told me that he thought Lloyd had died, probably from the diabetes, but he wasn't sure. It might have been from something else.

My father liked to watch a television show entitled *My World and Welcome to It,* which was a situation comedy loosely based upon the works of James Thurber. It starred William Windom as John Monroe, a cartoonist and author, and Lisa Gerritsen as his daughter. She wore a night brace. The family owned two dogs, one of which was a bloodhound.

One night, my father and I sat in the den in the Newtown Square house, watching the show on our black-and-white television, Playboy at his feet. The episode we watched that night was about the death of the bloodhound. Neither Monroe's wife nor his daughter understood the depth of the emotion that the man was feeling. When I turned to look at my father when the show was over, I was shocked to see that tears had rolled down his cheeks and that he was silently crying. I had never seen my father cry before. He wiped his eyes.

"Well," he said. "It's sad."

Sixteen years later, when he was dying of cancer, I saw him cry again. We were watching the film *My Dinner with Andre.* "A baby holds your hands," said Andre Gregory, "and then suddenly there's this huge man lifting you off the ground. And then he's gone. Where is that son?"

One spring day I'd been standing under a tree on the playground at the Alice Grim Elementary School when an arm wrapped around my neck and a moment later I found myself in a headlock, held fast to the hip of a boy named Brandon Coogan. "Let me go," I suggested, flailing. But Coogy wasn't leaning that way. He dragged me, instead, around the playground for fifteen or twenty minutes, as if I were some kind of northern pike and Coogy the world's luckiest fisherman.

In conclusion, Coogy threw me onto a kind of merry-go-round device on the playground, a flat circle that spun around an iron hub, where dear Mickey Lupin was patiently waiting to take things up to the Next Level. I don't even remember exactly how it happened, other than that I was trying to get away from Mickey, from Coogy, and in some awful way from my own self, but somehow I wound up *under* the spinning merry-go-round. This was good in the short run, since no one could get at me under there, but bad in the long, since once I had rolled under the thing, the only way out was through the space between the blacktop and the merry-go-round, where the legs of children dangled off the edge. Each time I tried to escape, the rotating series of booted feet were there to kick me back, boots whose impact was amplified by the speed with which the merry-go-round over my head was turning. In the end, I made good my escape, but only by enduring the kicks of what I came to see was virtually every member of my class, including the girls. Coogy was standing there as I finally crawled back to the daylight of the Grim School's playground. He took a good look at me and then said a single sentence, by way of summarizing the things that had come to pass.

"That's what you get," he said.

My father came into my room that night and inspected the damage. I had a torn lip and what would shortly blossom into a world-class shiner. "Thought you might want these, old man," he said. In his hands were a pair of small boxing gloves. They'd been his in the 1930s. The gloves were embroidered with the word CHAMP on the outside.

"When I was a boy," my father said, "people used to mess with me."

I looked at the antique baby boxing gloves in my hand. Learning how to box was the last thing I wanted. I slipped my hands inside the gloves. They were soft.

One night, Lloyd lay on a cot in my room. I tried to get him to talk about Marple Newtown, or his girlfriend, but he was strangely silent. In a corner of the room my Venus flytraps were silently digesting some hamburger. My plastic model of the human heart stood on my bookcase. By the dim glow of my night-light you could see the atria and the ventricles and the aorta and the vena cava.

"You're a lucky stiff," Lloyd said at last.

"Am I?" I said. I didn't feel lucky. I felt like I was cursed.

"Duh," said Lloyd.

There was silence for a while. But I had to ask.

"How am I lucky?" I asked.

"Because," Lloyd said, "you still have yours."

The windows were open, and from the woods that surrounded

the house came the thick threnody of Pennsylvania night: owls, cicadas, crickets. It was like a rain forest out there.

"I'm sorry," I said. It was the only thing I could think of. I still didn't know if we were talking about his father or his dog.

Earlier, Lloyd and I had walked up Sawmill Road with Playboy on a leash, my arm being gently pulled out of its socket, as the last of twilight dwindled around us. Playboy began to sniff around a path that led into the woods. He growled softly, and the hair on his back stood up. I looked into the dark forest. At the top of the hill, just barely visible, was one of the ruined mansions. One stone wall of a nineteenth-century barn stood there as well, along with—as I knew from exploring this place—the stone cellar of a vanished milk house without any walls around it whatsoever, a place into which, if you weren't careful, it was very easy to fall. And of course, the springhouse, the headwaters of the Thomas Run.

From the dark woods came Sandy Flash's whispered voice. *Death.*

Playboy growled again.

Then he bolted up the trail. The leash snapped out of my hand.

"No," I said. "Bad dog. Come!"

Playboy didn't look back. I wasn't expecting him to. Playboy didn't give a shit.

He bounded into the forest and disappeared.

Lloyd just nodded, unsurprised. "Toby used to do that, too."

We walked into the woods together, Lloyd and I. The sun was going down, and the woods were filled with long shadows and shocking sounds of croaking insects, a whole symphony of cicadas and crickets and other things whose names I did not know. The abandoned mansion in the woods looked as if it could fall over at any moment. Curtains blew from the windows. Most of the roof had fallen in. A voice said, "I love you."

Lloyd put one finger on his lips. Who would say such a thing, and in this place?

We crept around the sides of the old house. There was one person talking and another breathing heavily or gasping. They didn't know we were there. "Stop it," said one of them. "Don't be saying that."

The voices were coming from the old milk house, the outbuilding that by this point in time had devolved into a large, square, stone-lined hole in the ground. The two of them were sitting very close to each other, their faces one face. My parents kissed sometimes, but never like this. We'd been taught mouth-to-mouth resuscitation at school on a waxy dummy. There'd been a whole morning where we all stood in line, waiting our turn to bring the dummy back to life. You had to tilt her head back first.

"Wait," said one of the women. "Did you hear something?" They pulled away from each other. I couldn't see their faces. Along the tree line beyond the ruined milk house a Harley leaned on a kickstand. Something snapped in the woods—a twig beneath a boot. My heart pounded in my breast, although a breast wasn't what I had. There was a pulsing in the soft skin at the bottom of my throat.

"There's nothing there," said one.

After a while their faces drew together again. The women's legs dangled down into the hole. I wanted to get out of there. But something held me. The women made soft cat sounds in the insect dark.

The door of the old house behind us creaked, and I turned to look back. There was Playboy, peeing on the wall. The half-open door behind him moved gently back and forth upon its hinges.

I walked over to him and picked up his leash, which was still attached to his collar, trailing loosely on the ground. I patted him on the head.

I nodded to Lloyd, like, *Let's go.* Lloyd gave me such a look, like, *We could sit here watching lesbians make out with each other, and you want to go play with the dog?*

But then he relented, and we headed down the path together.

My family would leave this place in just another year or two. The descendants of Governor Earle sold that whole tract of land to developers. One weekend surveyors' posts began appearing in the forest, with red streamers attached to them. Then there were bulldozers and guys with chain saws. Governor Earle's ruined mansion was demolished, along with all of the old houses. Earle's Lake, where I'd caught brown trout with my cousin Peg, became a sewage treatment plant. The last time I drove down Sawmill Road, it looked like any other suburb in Delaware County. The new development was called Greene Countrie Village. The only sign of the former world was in the backyard of one of the McMansions, where the fireplace of the old house was still standing. Everything else was gone—the milk house, the springhouse, and the old stone ruin itself, of course. But the fireplace they left.

We got back to the house. My mother was making Shake 'n Bake chicken. My sister was in the basement, cleaning her tack. Lloyd shot himself up with some insulin and then sat down to practice the cello, Saint-Saëns's *The Swan.* My father came in and sat in his chair, listening. After a while he got down on his hands and knees and wrestled with the dog. It was such a strange scene—my diffident, gentle father rolling around with the snarling dalmatian, Lloyd's cello swooning with *The Swan,* the air redolent with Shake 'n Bake.

Afterward, my father lay on the floor, rubbing the dog's pink belly and stroking his ears. "You're the best dog," he told the dalmatian. "You're the very best dog."

And suddenly I was so angry I had to get up and leave. I went into my room and picked up an iron doorstop shaped like the *Santa Maria* and threw it against the wall. The ship clanked against the wall of my room and then fell onto the wooden floor. My ears rang. For a moment, Lloyd's bow lifted from his cello.

The pair of boxing gloves hung from the corner of my bed. I put them on but did not lace them up.

I sat there on the side of my bed looking at the gloves and the inscription on the back: CHAMP. The laces dangled down.

II

Sausage, 1973

My father shrugged. He's not much, he said.

My sister was going around and around. First the vertical planks, then the pair of Swedish oxers, then the diagonal double back over to the wall. Next: the combination, another plank, the in-and-out. A timer at one end of the ring counted off the seconds. There was a terrifying, ringing *knock* as Checkmate's hoof hit a fence rail, like a mallet ringing a wood block. The rail did not fall. There was a slow murmur from the grandstand as it became clear that she'd take over first place now if she completed the round without any faults. The horse thundered over the water jump, another vertical, a combination.

I could hear her encouraging Checky quietly as she raced toward the finish. *Come on, come on,* like a stage whisper. Now the oxers again, back to the in-and-out, and finally the set of jokers bearing the name of the sponsor, Anheuser-Busch.

By the old barns surrounding the ring waited the Clydesdales, hauling their ornate carriage. The huge, heavy horses shook their heads, the reins flapping against their broad, shining necks.

Cyndy crossed the finish line. "And we have a new leader," said the announcer as the grandstand went wild. Beyond the judge's booth rose a Ferris wheel, the flashing lights of the midway. *"Cyndy Boylan on Checkmate: no faults!"*

Everyone cheered. I turned to GI Joe. No, he was *not* a doll, he was an *action figure,* let's make that clear. He was happy, too, in his way. "Bravo Zulu," said Joe, by which he meant *Good job.*

Joe had his own way of talking. A lot of it was in code.

It was good that GI Joe gave my sister the old Bravo Zulu, because to me this endless circling was all the same. My complete indifference was awkward for my parents and, to a lesser extent, my sister, because their worlds revolved around the barn and the shows. My sister soared over obstacles on her horse as my parents sat in canvas-backed director's chairs ringside, drinking gin and tonics. Every day after school, my sister went out to the stables. On the weekends, there was a show on Saturday or Sunday, sometimes both, and they loaded up the maroon 1968 Impala station wagon and drove off to these events—in the countryside of southwest Pennsylvania, in the Brandywine Valley, in Delaware, in New Jersey, and in the Virginias, both West and regular.

While they were thus engaged, I stayed at home with Gammie and her friend Hilda and sometimes my aunt Gertrude, the seamstress.

Gammie brought along a handle of vodka and sang songs for me on the piano, including one called "Animal Fair."

The big baboon by the light of the moon was combing his auburn hair.

Hilda, a tiny woman from North Yorkshire, wore not particularly effective hearing aids. Sometimes, when Gammie started singing, she took them out entirely.

My aunt Gertrude worked at Lillian's Bridal Salon, sewing together veils and gowns. She'd been married to my uncle Frank for a couple of years, back in the 1950s, but then he'd dropped dead. When we were little, Aunt Gertrude had lived up in our attic. We used to hear her listening to bossa nova music up there.

She had another record she liked, Eddie Lawrence's "Old, Old Vienna." This song told the amusing story of an Austrian village wiped out by a landslide of strudel.

The narrator of the song heaved a sentimental sigh at the ballad's conclusion. *Ah!* he said. *Zat was Vienna!*

"I'm sorry we ignored you," my mother said to me on the phone, years later. Her voice quavered. "We were just so proud of Cyndy. She was so beautiful, on horseback. We loved watching her. But we forgot about you. It wasn't fair."

What Hildegarde was saying wasn't untrue, of course, and I'd spent no small amount of time in the intervening years grumbling about how I'd been ditched as a child, over and over again, so that they could drive off to watch my sister compete in horse shows. Indeed: that I spent so many hours listening to Gammie sing "Animal Fair" and eating hot dog stew was hardly fair.

But the truth of the matter is that I liked being alone. I woke up at dawn and headed out into the woods with Playboy. I explored the abandoned houses on the Earle estate. I fished for brown trout with my rod and reel in brightly trickling streams. I stood beneath the arch of a stone bridge and skipped stones upon Crum Creek. You could make the case for how sad it was, if you wanted, that my family was constantly giving me the slip. But if I were to be honest about it, I *liked* being ditched. Nothing made me happier than everyone else going away, leaving me to explore the universe with Playboy. In the end, Gammie and Hilda were just the price I had to pay for those blissful, silent hours in the forest with the dog, and after a certain point my parents didn't even bother with the formality of Gammie anymore and just trusted me to fend for myself. I mowed the lawn with the Sears mower, my nostrils thick with the smell of gasoline and fresh-cut grass, my ears ringing from the roar of the engine.

The elephant sneezed and fell on his knees, and that was the end of the monk.

"It was fine," I told my mother. "You did a good job." She did, too.

And she was right about my sister. She was beautiful on a horse.

Actually, she was beautiful off of a horse, too. Cyndy was a year and four months older than I, born in February 1957. She had long bright yellow hair, and blue eyes like my father, and a poise and confidence that you could not have found in me. While I was off talking military code with GI Joe and changing the oil in the riding mower, she was busy becoming a child prodigy. By the time she was thirteen, my sister was the top-ranked junior rider in the state of Pennsylvania. It was a rarefied world, the world of competitive show jumping and riding. But she was a star.

Checkmate and my sister were beautiful to watch. There was

something unworldly about them together, something that you could describe only as love or grace.

I hated horses, hated the way they dominated our family's lives, hated that the equestrian world so often required that I eat hot dog stew. So maybe, as the saying goes, I'm the wrong guy to ask.

But even I understood that there was something eternal about the gift my sister had been given. And given the rarity of this miracle, what else could I do except resent her for it, my heart filling with vanity and with hate.

In 1958 I had arrived on the scene two months prematurely, landing me in the hospital for a large chunk of my first year. My mother had had to come home without her baby. My father used to stop by the hospital and look in on mini me on his way home from work. "How's the boy?" my grandmother asked him.

Dad shrugged. "He's not much," he said.

Gammie told me this story, so is it true? I don't know.

Incredibly, on my eleventh birthday, we'd gone back to Whispering Winds. Now it seems like an odd choice, given our experience with Playboy. Surely it wasn't because we were such satisfied dog consumers that we gave them our business once more? Perhaps it was my mother's reality-defying optimism that led us there—although it's also hard to imagine my mother willingly agreeing to more dogs in her life.

None of it makes sense. All I can think is that we were hoping Playboy was the exception and that we could prove the goodness of the universe by buying another dalmatian and, by the object lesson of it *not* being as impossible as the older dog, show everyone that things did work out after all, that you could buy a dog from a certified American Kennel Club breeder and have it *not* chase motorcyclists and steal the entire Thanksgiving turkey off the counter.

I must have said I wanted a dog for my birthday, but I don't remember asking for one. Somehow we'd returned to Whispering Winds and returned with not one but two dalmatian puppies, one for me and one for my sister. Now everyone had a dog except my mother; or, looked at another way, my mother now had three dogs, plus my father and my sister and me.

Within a week, she was cleaning more dog shit off the floor with a scrub brush and a bucket of Top Job.

I named my dog Penny, after the younger daughter of the Robinson family in the television program *Lost in Space*. It was a show about a relatively normal family that, through no fault of its own, wound up crashed on an alien planet when their flying saucer got the wrong end of a meteor shower. My sister named her dog Chloe.

Penny had a hunger that could not be assuaged. We fed the dog Gaines-Burgers, which looked a little like pink ground beef arranged into patties, although there was something about the texture that suggested the burgers had been synthesized in an atomic research facility. Penny slathered down her Gaines-Burgers and then nosed Chloe aside and ate hers as well. Before the dogs were a year old, Penny was the size and shape of a beer keg and Chloe's ribs were visible beneath her spots. The dogs took on new names: Penny became Sausage. Chloe became Little.

And so we became a family of three dalmatians, each one slightly more insane than the one that had come before. Playboy, now that he was CEO of the dogs, became more unruly and belligerent than ever. Penny, meanwhile, lumbered enormously from one room to the next, looking for scraps. And Little was a flibbertigibbet: a will-o'-the-wisp, a clown.

It was clear early on that Penny was kind of a loser, an elephant seal of a creature haplessly waddling from room to room in hopes of finding a better world. In this quest she was disappointed.

My sister and I were not given to spending much time together during this era. Mostly we fought, with my sister—larger, stronger, and smarter—almost always the victor. Once, she pinned me to the basement floor, opened my mouth, and poured the entire contents of a sugar bowl into it until the grains sprinkled down the sides of my cheeks.

You might think this sounds cruel, but I can assure you I provoked her, like the time I filled her bed with rubber spiders and cold spaghetti. Given my talents in this arena, the punishment probably fit the crime.

The first game I really remember playing with my sister was something called hide-and-go-Penny. It was pretty much what it sounds like. We'd call her—"Here, Penny"—and the dog would wander in the general direction of the place she'd heard human voices, and then we'd hide. Enormous dotted Penny looked uncertainly around the room as my sister and I slipped off to another chamber. Then we called, "Here, Penny," and once more the dog would waddle off in search of us. Then we'd hide again.

I performed a monologue in the Voice of Penny. Imagine the voice like that of the possessed child in *The Shining*. It went like this: *I keep hearing people discussing this Penny. I wonder who it could be. She must really be a terrible, horrible creature, the things I hear about her. She must be a truly awful—*

Wait. Wait a minute. Wait.

I think—Wait. Oh no.

I'm Penny? Oh no. Oh no. Wait.

. . .

<u>*I'm*</u> *Penny.*

One day my father found a spot on his back. My mother assembled us all in the family room, with its zebra-striped paneling and the wagon-wheel chandelier, to have a serious conversation. Your father has malignant melanoma, she explained. They're going to take off the mole. If they get it all, he's going to be fine.

What if they don't get it all? I asked.

Walt Disney's animated film *One Hundred and One Dalmatians* was released in 1961. It was based on a 1956 novel by the British playwright Dodie Smith. Born in Lancashire in 1896, Smith moved to London in 1910, where as a young woman she wrote plays and acted, although the harsh realities of surviving as an artist led her in time to a day job at a furniture store. As an author, she didn't want people to know she was a woman at first.

Tell me about it.

She published under the name C. L. Anthony. When she was finally outed as female, a newspaper broke the scandalous news: SHOP-GIRL WRITES PLAY. She wrote eleven plays, nine novels, two screenplays, and four memoirs. The titles of her memoirs track a certain downward progression, from *Look Back with Love* (1974) to *Look Back with Mixed Feelings* (1978) and, later, to *Look Back with Astonishment* (1979). Her best-known play might be *Dear Octopus,* in which one character remarks, "The family—that dear octopus from whose tentacles we never quite escape, nor, in our inmost hearts, ever quite wish to." She also wrote a well-regarded novel entitled *I Capture the Castle*, which has been described as an inverted *Catcher in the Rye*, a story about a teenage heroine desperate to escape the tentacles of her own suffocating family but who is kept hostage, along with her stepmother and sister, in a crumbling, haunted mansion by her doomed father.

The last line of the novel is, *Only the margin left to write on now. I love you, I love you, I love you.*

I carried Penny around like an unusually heavy rag doll. Playboy wouldn't put up with being touched by human beings (except for my father), but Penny submitted. In time we would learn that she had a defective thyroid, which made her experience the world at a sloweddown pace (and was also responsible for her losing the hair on her tail, not to mention the brown goo that oozed endlessly from her eyeballs). In some ways the dog had the consciousness of a giant squid, some sort of deep-ocean creature that spent its days in the dark. At night I carried her into my room and put her under the covers and I put my arms around her, our two heads upon the pillow.

Sometimes, in the morning, I woke up to find that the brown goo that oozed out of Penny's eyes had stained the pillowcase as we slept.

My mother suggested that it might be better if Penny slept upon the floor. I looked at her as though she were crazy.

"But I *love* Penny," I observed.

"Poor Penny," my mother replied, and shook her head sadly.

This next part is hard to write, even fifty years later.

The great memoirist and provocateur Anne Lamott has famously written, "You own everything that happened to you. Tell your stories.

If people wanted you to write warmly about them, they should have behaved better."

But you can cause harm to people even when you write about them warmly. And I have written about plenty of people, including, on one occasion, my sister, in a manner that perhaps fell short when it came to warmth.

The problem is—we own our lives, sure. But our lives don't belong only to us.

And yet, we are here to tell our stories and in this way to make sense of our lives. So how do you tell a story when you know that telling it will bring other people sorrow? Is it better, in the end, to just be silent?

Like I said, maybe I'm the wrong guy to ask.

My sister was currycombing her horse, and then the horse broke loose. Had a bee stung him? Checkmate galloped suddenly down the driveway and into the road and was struck by a car and killed.

And so. Let me now draw the curtain on our family, as it was, and allow a few years to pass.

Time heals some of the wounds that the world gives us, but not all of them, and some we keep forever. Incredibly, a few hurt more the longer ago they happened.

It is true that it is this business of being hurt, and healing in the aftermath, that gives us our character, our strength and wisdom. And I say, Hooray for wisdom! Hooray for strength!

But which would you choose, if given the choice between wisdom and happiness? Is illumination really all that great a consolation for heartbreak?

Anyway, I know which one I'd pick, if given the choice.

Which I wasn't.

Now we are teenagers. Those odd children that we were—a nerd and a prodigy—have disappeared, or maybe it would be better to say *receded*.

We have moved from the house where I spent the long days wandering around a forest with Playboy and instead settled into a decrepit mansion on what is called the Main Line, the series of swanky suburbs outside of Philadelphia.

By the time we move, between my eighth- and ninth-grade years at school, the changes in our family are well in motion. My hair is growing longer, and I've swapped my plastic nerd Mr. Science glasses for little wire rims. I am a willowy, feline creature.

Incredibly, one of the moving men begins to flirt with me, under the belief that I am a hot, if flat-chested, teenage girl. But in this matter his hopes prove nugatory. When his discovery is made clear, he looks at me with anger and loathing, as if his disappointment is something I have somehow done to him on purpose.

My parents always told me the reason we moved was that the Earle estate had been sold to developers and that whole empire I once ruled in my splendid isolation was shortly to be transformed into lots of little subdivided lots. But I wonder, looking back, if perhaps that home was too synonymous with the people we had been and all at once—cruelly, randomly—stopped being?

In the summer of 1972, the Rolling Stones tour America, and our world bursts wide open. My sister comes home with *Hot Rocks,* and *Sticky Fingers,* and *Let It Bleed,* and suddenly the house is lousy with Mick Jagger. Cyndy develops an affection as well for Mott the Hoople, and the Who, and David Bowie. One night, we stay up late together to watch Dick Cavett interview Mick on TV. It is hard to say which one of them is more charming.

Also, there is *Jesus Christ Superstar,* which my rock-and-roll-hating father grumpily admits is a clever piece of music. Parts of it are in 7/4! he observes approvingly.

The house, in Devon, is haunted: by ghosts, by the residue of its legendary former occupants, the Hunts, and of course by us. Within a year or two, Playboy will also be among the dead, along with, heart-breakingly, my sister's dog, Chloe, who has some sort of malfunctioning pancreas, the direct result, I suspect, of the overbreeding that Disney's *One Hundred and One Dalmatians* makes endemic. To our new house, with its long, creaking stairs and many unoccupied, leaking rooms, we have brought Penny, who now waddles in and out of a dog door in order to squat, tremblingly, in a fenced-in area adjacent to the house. Every couple of days, my mother goes out to this place—she calls it "the kennel"—with a shovel and an aluminum bucket.

Here are the things we have not brought to Devon: The Venus flytraps. The rocket arsenal. My model trains. My clock shaped like an owl with the eyes that tick left, then tick right. The saltwater aquarium with my seahorses clinging by their tails to plastic seaweed.

In a storage room on the third floor, next to the room where I now live in a chamber covered with posters for the Allman Brothers Band, is a cardboard box filled with all of my sister's ribbons and trophies from her horse days. Her saddle is in the storage room, too.

One day, I climb out my sister's window in order to string speaker wire from her room to the stereo in the living room downstairs. Now my sister can listen to raucous rock-and-roll music right in her room, sometimes with the door closed. My parents, who live in the room across the hall from her, can now enjoy the not especially well muffled sounds of Alice Cooper. *Welcome to my nightmare,* says Alice.

My parents are not thrilled about my ingeniousness. Why would you do such a thing? my mother asks, as if by stringing speaker wire I have somehow broken some kind of unspoken promise to her.

The answer to this question, which I do not speak aloud, catches me by surprise.

Because I love her?

It is true that I have now swapped one dog for another—replaced Playboy with Penny. Likewise my identity as one kind of boy—*effeminate nerd*—has been upgraded to *nascent hippie*.

But even more unexpected, I have performed another kind of legerdemain. For as long as I could remember, I was a loner.

But now I am a brother.

I lived to make her laugh.

I became a merciless mimic. My voice was strangely elastic, and I found myself able to create, with eerie realism, impressions of a wide range of people: Richard Nixon, Johnny Carson, James Cagney—all of whom were the standard targets for "impressions" in 1973. But I was also able to create voices of my mother and father, several of my friends, even the girls that I loved. Sometimes I would call people up and pretend I was someone else.

But my primary audience was Cyndy. I developed a particular routine that she found entertaining, *The Hildegarde Time Show.* This involved climbing into the fireplace (which I pretended was a television) and narrating a show in which my mother somehow had become the anchorwoman of a program whose only purpose was announcing what time it was. "It's twelve twenty-seven," I would announce with a strange, beatific smile, and then just stare at the camera for a long, long time. Eventually I'd check my watch. "It's *still* twelve twenty-seven," I'd say.

My sister gradually assembles a group of cool friends. There's a girl named Lily, who is a year older than everyone else, the result of being held back at her school for reasons never quite specified. There's a group of boys who go to the Episcopal Academy who act in plays and perform in rock-and-roll bands. They all come over to the house, and my sister sits me down in front of them for entertainment. "Okay, Jimmy," she says. "Have at it."

In no time at all I am inventing songs for them on the piano or doing imitations. I perfect what I call the "Imitation Imitation," which is, for instance, Bob Dylan imitating Richard Nixon; or Marlon Brando imitating Gypsy Rose Lee. Inevitably, this evolves into the "Imitation Imitation Imitation": JFK imitating Johnny Carson imitating Dudley Do-Right. And so on.

I am highly entertaining. Everyone laughs and laughs at my incredible antics.

This is very different from staying home with my Venus flytraps and eating hot dog stew with Gammie while Cyndy braided her horse's tail out at the stables. It is hard to believe that this other world took place just a couple of years ago.

I think it makes my parents a little sad, that my sister's world suddenly revolves around me instead of them. A lot of the time now, if there are fights, my sister and I are on one side and they are on the other. Some of the clever, ironic things I say don't make any sense, at least not to them. In just a couple of years, my parents find that their children have become something more like strangers to them—with secrets, and in-jokes, and unspoken understandings.

Sometimes my sister and I laugh so hard that we fall upon the floor, unable to speak or move, just shaking so hard that it is not clear if we are going to be able to survive our own happiness. It makes it hard to breathe.

My friend John leaned toward me conspiratorially. "The walls are breathing," he explained.

An album entitled *Tubular Bells* played on the stereo. This included a section in which a caveman sang: *Stuccotowfrash dow wonawow. Stuccotowfrash dow wonaw.*

A half a dozen hippies ate Meow Mix at the kitchen table, a piece of furniture that had giant claws for feet. The house was lousy with teenagers tripping on LSD, although neither my sister nor I was partaking. Cars were parked at crazy angles out on the street. Moey had dropped a boulder through the windshield of Lisa Boyer's yellow Volkswagen Beetle.

My parents were in New Orleans. They had decided that my sister and I, at sixteen and fifteen, were old enough to trust for a few days without having a babysitter.

A girl walked through the room with a collection of butter pats arranged on a tray like cheese. "Butter pats?" said the girl, whose spaghetti-strap top suggested a phrase from Scripture: *Her cups runneth over.* Her breasts were an absolute wonder—proof, just as Benjamin Franklin had once remarked about the provenance of beer, that there is a God and that he wants us to be happy. "Who would like some pats of butter?"

My sister came down the back stairs. "Red alert in your room," she said.

"Roger," I said.

I left the room of breathing walls and ascended the long, creaking stairs. After a couple of years, I reached my bedroom door, which was closed. Dim light shone through the transom.

"Rrrrr," came a growling voice.

"Hello?" I said. My door was locked. "Who's in there?"

Someone barked in reply.

Downstairs, Moey was fighting with my friend Lemonshit. "You don't want to do this," suggested my friend Link, observing the melee. "We know you're good people."

"Fuck you," said Moey, taking another swing at Lemonshit. Blood ran from Lemonshit's nose. In the dining room, Oliver Brown's girlfriend sat down on the arm of one of the dining room chairs, but it wasn't the kind of arm you should sit on, as she came to understand when it snapped in two beneath her.

"Uh-oh," said she.

"You're not the kind of person who does this," Link explained to Moey. Moey lived in a place called Garrote Hill. He was the size of a vending machine.

"Yeah?" said Moey. "Watch."

In the garish living room—its walls painted black—a girl named Onion was playing the *Moonlight Sonata*.

The week before, Onion had been to an abortion clinic, and the receptionist had looked up at her and said, by way of greeting, *You again.*

"Can you open the door, please?" I said to whoever was in my room.

But the reply came only in the form of barking. Whoever it was that was in my room was apparently holding Penny hostage. Or vice versa.

There were four rooms on the third floor, plus the bathroom. My room was the only one that was used for anything. The others were a storeroom, and a guest room, and an empty room with some broken furniture. Sometimes my friends and I painted the walls in the empty room with tempera paints. I had drawn the silhouette of a cunicular shape against a horizon, along with the caption THE ENORMOUS RABBIT SEEN FROM A DISTANCE.

The people who lived in the house before us used to keep a monkey in the bathroom. The monkey's name was Jesus. Because when people opened the bathroom door and beheld the monkey, they would shout, *Jesus!* One time, Jesus gave birth to a baby monkey in the sink. It didn't make it.

"Hello?" I said. It felt sad to knock on my own bedroom door. "Who's there?"

Then there was a growl and a bark. Poor Penny. Then there was another growl, like a human imitating a dog. "Lily, is that you?"

Her little sister, Starr, had died of cystic fibrosis a year before. Lily had driven me out to the St. David's churchyard and visited the grave. We made a daisy chain together as we sat around the grave.

"Hey," I said. "Can you open the door?" From downstairs, three stories below, came the sound of glass shattering. Moey and Lemonshit were still working things out.

"Rrrrr," she said, and at this moment, from the other side of the door, Lily's voice was indistinguishable from that of my dog, a bloated creature who did not know where she was.

At Whispering Winds I had found Penny sleeping under a pee-stained sheet of *The Philadelphia Inquirer.* She looked at me with soft, weary eyes.

It's been said before that in any relationship, the person who cares least is the person with all the power. In my relationship, that person was a dog.

I brought her treats. I invited her into the *Gemini* capsule I had built in the corner of my room—I'd converted it from a *Polaris* submarine I'd bought from the back pages of a comic book. I lavished her with affection I had never received from Playboy. I picked her up like a rag doll and carried her everywhere.

Penny didn't like any of this. I think she was indifferent to me as an individual, as she was to all humans, but she definitely didn't like being picked up and carried, and if it was a choice between being kissed on the ears or being left alone to lie on her side passing gas, it's clear enough what she would have preferred. I figured if I kept being sweet to Penny all the time, eventually her heart would open, and she would love me as I loved her. No one told me this is never how it works.

In London many years later, in a Tom Stoppard play, I'd hear Glenn Close say, "Gallons of ink and miles of typewriter ribbon expended on the misery of the unrequited lover; not a word about the utter tedium of the unrequiting." It must have been tedious, for Penny, to be loved by me.

I know at times, in thinking of my mother, how tedious it was for me to be loved by her.

From deep in the house I heard the sound of *Tubular Bells* again. *Stuccotowfrash dow wonawow. Stuccotowfrash dow wonaw.*

"Lily? Can you open the door?" I said.

There was a long silence as she thought this over. "Open the door," she said regretfully.

I knocked on the door a little more, but Lily had decided, like HAL 9000, that "this conversation can serve no purpose anymore."

I had loved Lily for a long time, although I knew she didn't have any interest in me.

We drove around in her car sometimes, visited her sister's head-stone, picked flowers. One time, she looked at me and said, "You would make a great chick."

It wasn't what I wanted the girl I loved to say.

"No, seriously," she said. "We should make you into a girl some-time. Shave your legs. I could do your makeup."

"I don't think so," I said, my voice trembling, and hot tears burned in my eyes. I wanted her to love me, not least because I hoped that love would transform me. But it wasn't a girl I wanted her to trans-form me into: it was a boy without shadows.

Instead she just looked at me and thought, as my father had thought so long ago, *He's not much.*

There I stood, in front of my own locked door. I had dreamed of getting Lily into my bedroom for a long time. But I'd always assumed that if I got her there, I'd be in the room with her at the same time.

Before the party began, Lily had promised to paint a mural in my room. She was good with paint. I figured if I couldn't make out with her, at the least I could have her draw on my walls. It wasn't sex, but as my mother liked to say, "it wasn't nothing."

I got a chair from the storeroom and put it in front of my door, then climbed up to the transom. With one hand I pushed the transom window all the way open, then I leaned into the room like an orangutan and reached down on the other side of the door with my long arms. My father had once said I had "arms like a willow tree," which I thought was nice, but I don't think he meant it as an actual compliment. I slid the dead bolt open, then climbed back out of the transom, hopped back on the ground. And opened the door.

I gazed around my bedroom. There was a lot to take in, like evidence at a crime scene. In the middle of the room upon the floor Lily lay there with her eyes closed and a big happy smile upon her face. On the floor nearby: Penny, aka Sausage, brown goo streaming from her eyes. And all around the room were pieces of evidence pertaining to the crime: the wall where the mural was to have been created bore the face of a sad-faced girl. She was surrounded by flowers, and lizards, and things that looked like breasts with wings. A pair of hands erupted out of a field.

"Lily," I said, bending to her. I touched her cheek.

Her eyes opened, and she looked at me with wonder, as though her heart were going to come out of her mouth and the two of us were going to eat it together.

"I knew you would come back," she said, and then reached forward and put her arms around me.

I wanted to hold her in my arms, and now my wish had come true, although—following what would turn out to be the recurring pattern for my wishes in the years to come—it had come true ironically, the thing I had wished for delivered, but in circumstances completely unlike the ones I had desired. Yes, she loved me, and she missed me, and she wanted to kiss me. But only because she thought I was her own sister, returned to her from the dead.

I wasn't who she thought.

A few weeks later, I came downstairs to find my mother and father by the fireplace, Sausage on the floor.

They'd found out what we'd been up to in their absence, of course, although my sister and I had tried nobly to hide some of the damage. We swept up the glass from the windshield of the car shattered by Moey when he threw the rock through it. We glued the arms back on the living room chairs. We dug the candle wax out of the ashtrays and returned the empty keg to the Bottle & Can. I painted over the unfinished mural that Lily had begun in my bedroom, wiped as much paint as I could off of the furniture. We tried to cover our tracks. But it was all in vain.

They weren't angry, they said. They were just very, very disappointed.

I would think these words many years later as I stood before the statue of Abe Lincoln in his memorial in D.C., the Great Emancipator's sad visage staring down at me. I wanted to apologize to Honest Abe for everything, starting with the assassination. But I just felt bad. That look in his eyes was both piercing and noble, and so wounded.

It was the same expression I now saw on my father's face. I figured Dick and Hildegarde were going to review some of the atrocities that had gone down on my watch, maybe starting with that nearly topless chick who'd walked around serving people pats of butter on a tray. "Hey, Dad," I said. "Are you okay?"

My father nodded. But he couldn't talk.

"Is this about the cancer?" I said. They'd taken off the mole, grafted part of my father's leg onto his back. "What's going to happen?"

The living room was a kind of graveyard of stuff, filled with the baby grand piano on which one of my party guests had puked and some oil paintings of street scenes in Paris: the Place de la Concorde in the rain, a bridge near Notre-Dame cathedral. There was an off-white love seat and two green wing chairs gathered around a fireplace. On the mantel were small porcelain figures of American birds: a robin, a blue jay.

"The doctors aren't sure," my mother said, "if they got it all."

I met Shannon at a coffeehouse at the Bryn Mawr Presbyterian Church. On Saturday nights people played coal-mining songs in the crypt. I gave Shannon and her friends Cynthia and Cynthia a ride from the crypt to someone's house. Shannon and Cynthia were in the back seat of my parents' Oldsmobile Omega, and Cynthia was up front. Shannon was an actress. As I drove through the farmland of Pennsylvania, she performed a monologue. The Cynthias and I laughed so hard I had to pull the car over because the tears in my eyes made it impossible to drive.

She recited Dorothy Parker poems. She did imitations. I told her I did imitations, too. She said hopefully, *Do you?*

I dropped Shannon off at her house, and then Cynthia off at hers, and then Cynthia off at hers, and then I got home and climbed the squeaking stairs to my room. Penny lifted her head. *Well?* she said.

I met someone, I told the dog.

Yeah well, said the dog. *Don't get your hopes up.*

A few weeks later, I picked Shannon up at her school, and we went out for dinner at a place called Winstons, which was a restaurant in Bryn Mawr. Shannon ordered French onion soup. I sat on my side of the table and watched her lift strands of gooey melted cheese to her mouth. "It's a mess," she said.

A couple of times a week I would call Shannon on the phone, and we would talk for hours. She had trouble with her parents. Her mother was a colorful, larger-than-life woman who, on one occasion, came to Shannon's school on Parents' Day wearing a miniskirt and go-go boots.

Shannon was tall and thin and had straight brown hair that fell halfway down her back. Unlike my other friends, Shannon didn't do drugs or drink. She was an actress—in the years to come I would see her in *A View from the Bridge;* and *You Can't Take It with You;* and *The Mousetrap.* There was something of Katharine Hepburn about her, although she was less imperious; at the heart of all her talent was a mixture of kindness and fire.

One night Shannon and I were back at my house. Penny lay on the bed, taking in the situation. I told Shannon about the world that now appeared to have passed, the world in which I was the loner within a family whose life revolved around horses, about the way I resented always being left behind but how I also treasured my solitude. She didn't say anything in reply at first, but then she said that she understood what it was like to be an outsider in your own family.

We got in the Omega, and just before I started up the engine, I leaned over and kissed her on the lips.

I have forgotten a lot of things, but I haven't forgotten that. She raised one hand and touched my cheek. It was nice.

All these years later, it still puts me in mind of that poem by Leigh Hunt (slightly altered for the occasion):

> *Say I'm weary, say I'm sad,*
> *Say that health and wealth have miss'd me,*
> *Say I'm growing old, but add,*
> *Shannon kiss'd me.*

Then she explained that she liked me, but she didn't like me like *that.*

I drove her home. When I got back to the house, it was quiet. The stairs creaked beneath my feet as I ascended. I sat down on the bed and put my face in my hands. Penny looked up at me, then lowered her sad, dotted face into my lap.

What did I tell you? said the dog. *I told you not to get your hopes up.*

My father had bought four tickets to the farewell performance of Arthur Rubinstein at the Academy of Music, with Eugene Ormandy conducting. There wasn't a lot that brought us all together anymore, but classical music came close. For his part, Rubinstein was back where he started, having made his professional debut in 1906 with the Philadelphia Orchestra at Carnegie Hall. Now into his eighties, Rubinstein was taking his leave. We would never see his like again.

But that day I told my parents I didn't want to go. Even my sister thought this was weird. "What are you going to do, just stay in this big house by yourself all night?"

Yes, in fact. That was pretty much the idea.

In spite of the fact that I had at last gained Cyndy as a friend, some things in me ran pretty deep. Wanting to be alone was one of them.

The other was the thing I could not discuss, even with her. I could not admit it even to myself, and to this day I cannot explain it to you, I suspect, in any way that would give you satisfaction. All I know is that the gentle voice that had whispered to me as a child, *You are not you,* had not grown softer. As adolescence advanced, and the world of men and women divided before me, it could not have been clearer to me that I was on the wrong shore of that ocean.

That conflict was, of course, the thing that helped to fire up my imagination, that made me such a furious generator of blarney. It made me tremendously entertaining, in my sad-faced, goofball fashion.

But it also made it impossible to reach another soul, or to be reached. How is it possible to be in love, to be at your most naked and vulnerable with another person, if all the while you know that you are lying to her?

I knew what the price would be if I ever spoke this truth aloud. I would lose my family; I would never be loved; I would be beaten. Killed, quite possibly, depending.

And so I kept my silence, in the manner I had been taught.

It was only on nights like this, when I was at last alone in the giant haunted house, that I could come out.

My father tried to hide his hurt, but he did not succeed. The piano was the thing that, even now, still bound us. After all, the Cable-Nelson upon which I played had once belonged to him, back in the 1940s when *he* had been the life of the party. I watched the three of them get into the Impala in their orchestra clothes and drive off. I would never hear Arthur Rubinstein play the piano live, in Philadelphia or in any other place.

I heard the sound of the car going up Chester Road and then silence. Penny looked at me. *What are you going to do?* she asked. *If you're not going to the orchestra?*

You know what I'm going to do, I replied.

A week or two later I went out to the swimming pool with a grapefruit knife. I sat down on the diving board and looked at it. It wasn't all that sharp. Gammie used it on Christmas mornings to segment the grapefruit, which she then doused with a shot of vodka and a maraschino cherry.

The night was full of sound. It wasn't as thick with the threnody of cicadas and other night creatures as the woods of Newtown Square had been, but it was still loud. I imagined myself falling into the pool, the knife dropping from my hand. The blue water would turn purple if I did it. I sat there on the diving board for a long time, imagining that color.

Then I went back inside. I washed the knife and then dried it with a Colonial Williamsburg dish towel and then I put it back in the drawer and climbed the stairs again. I knocked on my sister's door. "Are you awake?" I said.

She was reading a book by Gurdjieff. "Hey, little brother," she said.

I came in and sat on the floor of her room. She had a wall-to-wall shag rug with black and white threads. I leaned against the wall. I didn't know what to tell her. The tears hovered in my eyes, but I did not want her to see them fall.

"What's going on?" she asked.

"Why does everybody hate me?" I asked her.

"Everybody doesn't hate you," she said. "People just think you're weird."

"I'm not weird," I said. "Am I?"

She put her book down. "This is about Shannon, isn't it."

I shrugged. I didn't even know she knew about her.

"You really liked her, didn't you."

I didn't know what to tell her. I just sat there, not crying.

Then: "Hey, Jimmy," she said. "Do the *Time Show*."

I made the face I made when I was imitating my mother. "It's twelve twenty-seven," I said, and stared at her without blinking.

Within the year, my sister would be gone. It would be off to Carleton College, in Minnesota, for her, where she'd study dance and child development. She would never live in this room again.

"It's *still* twelve twenty-seven," I said.

When my sister went to college, I wrote her a note and put it inside a cream-colored envelope and marked it OPEN ON PLANE. Which she did. On it, I'd written, *You don't know what you've got till it's gone.*

Now it was just my parents and me in the big house, plus Penny, aka Sausage.

One night while they were out, I drifted out into the hallway. I forget what I was wearing, but I'm sure it was lovely.

I sat down at the baby grand piano and sang "Brokedown Palace" by the Grateful Dead. As I played I thought a little more about Shannon. Then I stopped playing. That song made a good case for accepting the truth that lovers come and go. But I wasn't in the mood for that particular message.

Penny stood up and growled. Something creaked at the top of the stairs. A heavy footstep thudded on the landing, then another. The hair on Penny's back rose up like a Mohawk. She growled again. The footsteps started down the stairs. I sat there at the piano, waiting.

The footsteps came halfway down, then paused. I couldn't see this place from where I was sitting, but if the thing crossed the empty place, it would come into my view with its next step. Penny looked at the stairs, frozen, growling.

"Who's there?" I said. *You wanted to see* Ba-boing!, *sir, and now you have seen him.*

There was no response, but I knew she was there, some lost soul watching me with longing.

I sat there for a long time, my arms full of goose bumps, my heart pounding. I wanted to get the hell out of the haunted house, but dressed like this? There was nowhere to go.

I started playing the piano again. "The Daring Young Man on the Flying Trapeze." *Once I was happy but now I'm forlorn.*

When I finished, Penny was lying back down on the floor. I got up and looked up the stairs. There was nothing there that you could see.

————

Just before the end of the school year, Shannon's school put on a talent show. It was 1976, the year of the American Bicentennial, and the centerpiece of the show was a group called the Belles of Liberty. I was seventeen. The Belles of Liberty was a group of about twenty-five girls on roller skates, including Shannon, who wore red-white-and-blue uniforms and sang while they skated.

For the talent show, the girls at Shipley got my friend Bunting to act as emcee, and he introduced each of the acts as they came up. There was Lisa Trousdale, who sang "Take Me Home, Country Roads" on the guitar, and Shell Stockhousen, who had a ventriloquist's dummy. There was Sarah Marshall, who juggled. Maria Henderson sang "Comes a Train of Little Ladies" from *The Mikado*.

The climax of the show was this: Bunting was to introduce Zero and our other friends Darryl and Larry. Larry had left school earlier that year after he unexpectedly punched out all the walls in his room. We didn't know why. The boys were going to be doing some sort of comedy routine—specifically *making fun of my mother*—during the middle of which I was to jump out of the audience and say, You guys really have a lot of nerve, I think the girls who've been putting on this show deserve an apology. At which point I was going to *throw a shaving cream pie into Darryl's face*. The Belles of Liberty would then roll out on the stage, each one with a cream pie, and everyone would throw them at each other while "The Stars and Stripes Forever" played on the loudspeakers.

At the appointed hour I was sitting in the crowded auditorium, surrounded by girls, listening to my friends do their act. At the last minute, though, they'd cleverly changed the object of their derision from an abstract one—my mother—to something more immediate. That would be me.

My friends came out on the stage and said, "Hey, that Jimmy Boylan's a real fag!"

I sat there in the audience. I guessed this was my cue.

Some of the girls nearby were already looking at me, wondering why I wasn't saying anything.

So I stood up and I said, "Hey, what's the big idea? You really have a lot of nerve. I think you owe everybody here an apology!" This was supposed to be really funny, but in fact there were tears in my voice as I spoke the words. No one was laughing.

I walked up onto the stage. It was really quiet.

Then Darryl hit me with a pie. I was blinded by pie even before I got to the pie table at center stage. Darryl creamed me so hard that I could literally see nothing, and I was unable to wipe the frosting out of my eyes.

And then the Belles of Liberty rolled in from offstage. I couldn't see them, but I heard them. There were twenty-five girls onstage in roller skates, and everybody was throwing pies. "The Stars and Stripes Forever" started playing on the PA.

Another unfortunate thing that had happened was that Darryl had hit me so hard with the pie that my nose began to bleed. I stumbled around the stage, my arms outstretched, a blind thing.

I stood in the middle of the stage at an all-girls school, in a spotlight, sightless, my face covered with white frosting. From my nose a bright red river of blood gushed into the white cream. All around me orbited two dozen girls on roller skates, including Shannon, the girl for whom I'd written my first poem. The music of John Philip Sousa played overhead.

Pies flew through the air, aimed first at the Belles of Liberty, then at the audience. People started screaming. I heard the sound of folding chairs overturning as the audience fled toward the exits. Some of the Belles of Liberty lost control and roller-skated off the edge of the stage and landed on the folding chairs. Others wiped out onstage and lay on their backs with the wheels on their skates still spinning. Someone else grabbed on to the curtain to keep from falling, and there was the sound of material ripping. Part of the curtain fell down. I took off my glasses to try to wipe my eyes again and they slipped out of my hand and fell onto the floor.

There was the sound of glass breaking as a girl careened by on roller skates. "Help," she said. "I can't stop."

After the debacle, we all went into the girls' gymnasium and took showers with our clothes on, washing off the pie. It was a big party, showering fully dressed with Shannon and the girls. Later, I wrapped myself up in a towel and headed over to Larry's house with Zero and Bunting, where we changed clothes and listened to the Grateful Dead perform the Marty Robbins tune "El Paso."

We drank Pabst Blue Ribbon out of sixteen-ounce cans and had a good laugh about what had happened at the talent show. We were boys and we had created a giant catastrophe in public. *Out of control!* said Doober.

I didn't feel all that good. I remembered sitting on the diving board of the swimming pool holding that knife, imagining the feeling of the point. Did I turn to my friends and say, *Hey. You hurt my feelings!*

No, I did not. That wasn't the way things were done among my people. There was a big hole in the wall from the night Larry punched out his room. We didn't talk about that, either. In the country of boys, there was no language for speaking of such things, save for the emblems of cream pies and of beer.

One little kiss, and Felina, goodbye.

My sister and I were sitting in my room, listening to "My Favorite Things." She was back from college. In my bed against the wall, Penny lay enthroned like Jabba the Hutt. She was beginning to show her age—Penny, that is. "You see that?" Cyndy said. "That's your dog." She smiled from ear to ear, to make sure I grasped her meaning: that whatever kind of weird this weird dog was, it was a direct result of answering to me.

Penny gave us that look again, the one that suggested, *Who is this Penny everyone keeps discussing? She sounds like such a terrible*—

"I'm serious," Cyndy said. "Take a good, hard look. *That's* your dog."

"I know it," I said, but what I knew in my heart, and what gave me an endlessly lingering shame, was this:

I'm Penny.

I did not know it then, but after my sister went off to Carleton I'd never quite have that relationship with her again. College would change us both, of course, in different ways. That's what it's supposed to do, of course. If you leave college resembling in any way the person you were when you first arrived, that college has failed you.

We would have other relationships in the years to come, as we morphed from one self to the next. If we'd been enemies as children, and friends as teenagers, there were plenty of other variations dead ahead: college boy, married woman, punk rocker, boyfriend, mother, hipster, expatriate, orphans, little old ladies.

I climbed the stairs, oblivious to the future, and arrived in my room. Everything in the old house was so quiet. To the left was the wall where once Lily had painted a mural of hands erupting from a field. To the right was the table with my stereo, upon which Cyndy and I had listened to Jethro Tull, Neil Young, John Coltrane. Outside my window was a tall pine tree that in just a few years lightning would strike during the heart of a storm, the electricity crackling halfway down the trunk in a blinding flash, as I clutched my dog like a life preserver.

Penny lay in my bed, her head upon my pillow.

"Down," I said. Penny opened one eye. *Seriously?* "Down," I said again.

Penny couldn't believe it. *Now? After all this time, you're changing the prime directive?*

"I'm not kidding, you sleep on the goddamned floor, Penny," I said.

Fine. Penny rolled her eyes, got herself up on all fours, and heaved herself resentfully onto the floor.

There'd been a time when I had carried my dog around like a rag doll, so deep was my love for her. Then the years had passed, and Penny had failed to keep up.

I had loved my sad, gelatinous dog with all my heart, for years and years, as I glued together models of the human brain and heart, as I raised Venus flytraps in a leaking aquarium. But then one by one I put the things of my childhood aside, and Penny was one of them. She wasn't cool enough for the person I was trying to become.

It wasn't that I didn't have love in my heart anymore. But the object of that love had changed.

I felt bad about it all and bent down to hold my poor old dog, my fingers running down her spotted ears, her lumpy coat. "It's okay, sweetie," I said. "You're a good girl." Her sad tail thumped against the floor. "You are. You're a good girl."

Only the margin left to write on now. I held her in my arms, as if she were already gone, as if all these days had long since become a distant memory.

"Poor Penny," I said.

III

Matt the Mutt, 1979

I had a dog like that once, the man said.
Now I got a bird.

Holy shit! It's *Matt the Mutt!* He's here! He's there! He's got
Penny in a corner! He's got his front paws on her back! What's he
doing? Tee-*haw*, Matt the Mutt! Now he's satisfied, and he's off: trot-
ting down the hall, running down the staircase. Wait, what's this? He's
paused on the second-floor landing—he's lifting his leg, and whoo-hoo!
He's whizzing right there on the wall! Matt the Mutt cannot be stopped!
Was that the back door? *Look out below!* He's running down the stairs
two steps at a time, arriving in the mudroom precisely in time to attack
my father, who's lumbering through the door. Dad had hoped to sneak

into the house without Matt the Mutt hearing about it, but *Matt the Mutt cannot be stopped!* He's *leaping into the air* and barking and pushing back upon my father's shoulders with both paws before falling back onto the floor and then *leaping once more* while barking and trying a second time to tackle my father and bring him to the floor. My mother's footsteps are coming swiftly, but not swiftly enough. Matt the Mutt leaps into the air again, barking and snarling. Dad is trying to ward him off with his briefcase. Dad is not succeeding.

"No," my mother says, reaching for the dog's collar. "No!"

Matt the Mutt doesn't like being hauled off of my father, and now he's barking at Hildegarde, who's put her hands over her ears. My father is shouting something at her, but she can't hear him, what with the barking and the covered ears. Matt the Mutt bounces into the air again and shoves my father against the door! Dad puts his briefcase down. Matt the Mutt raises one leg and pisses on it.

"Noo," says my mother. My father reaches for his briefcase, but he gets dog piss on his hand, and now Dad is yelling and my mother is shouting and Matt the Mutt is barking some more and leaping into the air.

Upstairs, in the library, Penny looks languidly up from the place where she lies and thinks, *Lord of my love, to whom in vassalage thy merit hath my duty strongly knit, to thee I send this written embassage, to witness duty, not to show my wit.*

Meanwhile, at Wesleyan University, where I am now a senior, Donna and I have reached my dorm room, and we kiss to say good night, and the kiss goes on for a while, and it's all very sweet. Donna has big brown eyes. She says, "The thing is, I don't have my diaphragm. Can you wait while I go and get it?"

"Your diaphragm," I say to her. I'm in a tight spot. Because of course I really like Donna, and making out with her is really great. But I don't love her, at least not with all my heart and soul. So I'm of two minds about what—if I'm understanding Donna's suggestion properly—is her proposal that we have actual sex.

"Yes," says Donna. "It's back at the house."

"Well," I say. "Well-dee-well-dee-well."

At Wesleyan I have inexplicably become cool, in part because I have both the hair and the glasses of John Lennon, who at that exact moment is not yet dead. I have a radio show during which I simultaneously play, on twin turntables, the Grateful Dead's "Dark Star" as well as T. S. Eliot reading "Burnt Norton." In my sophomore year, I write and produce a radio serial entitled *Squid Family*, which becomes very popular among a certain demographic. I play the college carillon each day at noon and feature theme songs from 1960s television shows, including *F Troop* and *The Brady Bunch*.

Sometimes I play the Christian hymn "How Can I Keep from Singing?" It would be a long time before I come to terms with my faith. In order to save face among my brethren and sisthren, I suggest that my hope that there is a force of love greater than ourselves is mostly ironic. In this way, I sneak by.

> *My life flows on in endless song;*
> *Above earth's lamentation,*
> *I hear the sweet, tho' far-off hymn*
> *That hails a new creation;*
> *Thro' all the tumult and the strife*
> *I hear the music ringing;*
> *It finds an echo in my soul—*
> *How can I keep from singing?*

I play piano and the Autoharp in coffeehouses and sing songs that I have written, including "Mr. Rogers Does the Puppets' Voices" and "Just a Bunch of Assholes from Outer Space." I am tremendously entertaining.

It is natural to assume that someone as entertaining as this is having loads and loads of sex. In fact, it is so natural that the fact that I have, in fact, had sex only once so far is a possibility that has not occurred to any of the women who are drawn to my questionable character. And the longer this goes on, the more impossible it is to explain to a potential lover that I'm reluctant to proceed with this project because I, like, don't actually know what I'm doing. Plus, the true love thing. There are a lot of obstacles.

The summer before, I had made love for the first time with another girl named Donna—if you can call an experience that was shorter in duration than the roll of summer thunder *making love*. Still, I loved Donna (London Donna, let us call her, to differentiate her from College Donna); she was the first person I had really fallen in love with since Shannon and the first woman to love me in return. I don't know why I was such a miser when it came to giving my heart away. In my entire life I have had sex with fewer people than the number of dogs I owned.

I don't know, maybe I was just scared. What would happen if we had sex and the next day she didn't love me anymore? What would we do then?

Being in love, to me, was a thousand times more important than having sex.

Years later, when I finally emerge as female, everyone will say they are shocked. *Shocked!*

It is already clear that, at age twenty-one, I am less successful at being in love than Matt the Mutt.

Or, to be more exact about it, it's that he does not conflate love with sex. He takes what he wants, without any sense of guilt. Matt the Mutt does not know what second thoughts are. All he knows is that joy is for the taking. I, on the other hand, will toss and turn over the question of love, whether I am deserving of it, whether I am right to ask it of another. It's not that I don't like sex; even my abbreviated experiences thus far confirm my suspicion that this business could, potentially, be a lot of fun. But unlike Matt, I didn't want to share it with just anybody, even someone I like as much as College Donna. Even at this young age I have already set the bar incredibly high—no sex without love, no love without soul.

I'm probably hardwired to experience the world in this way, although there are times when I wish I were not. It would have been a lot easier, to live a life without regret.

Most of the boys I knew at Wesleyan had a lot more in common with Matt the Mutt than they did with me.

"Maybe," I said to College Donna, "we should just call it a night. It's been so great." We had spent the evening listening to the music produced by the college's Javanese gamelan orchestra, that being the fashion at the time.

"Oh," said Donna, trying to hide the fact that I had crushed her. "Oh, okay." I don't think it occurred to her, in a million years, that my keeping her at arm's length was not about my not desiring her but about a lack of faith in myself.

I kissed her again, now that we'd come to this agreement. "Well, well," I said. "Well-dee-well-dee-well."

"Good night, James," said Donna with a sigh, and headed off toward her house. I stood in my door and watched the empty hallway for a few moments.

Many years later, a colleague of mine at *The New York Times,* another

Wesleyan alumna, expressed disbelief that I hadn't had sex at college, where she too had briefly been a member of the team of women hoping for a whack at James Boylan. "If you never had sex at Wesleyan, it wasn't for lack of opportunity," she said.

"I know," I told her. "I had plenty of opportunity. I just didn't have any motive."

I thought I was all done with the business of not having sex for the evening, when from across the hallway, a dorm-room door swung open, and there, all sleepy, was my friend Lucy, a bighearted, Camel-smoking, slow-talking architecture student. She had glasses almost exactly like mine. "Jaaames," she said, and raised one eyebrow.

Meanwhile, back in Pennsylvania.

My mother belongs to a group of ladies who play bridge. They come over to our house every six weeks or so, to play cards and to eat cucumber sandwiches and to drink gin and tonics in the middle of the day. The doorbell rings. The back door creaks open. "Hildegarde?" calls Mrs. Towson, one of the neighbors.

Hildegarde has told her friends not to walk in unless she herself has opened the door, but most of the women in her circle ignore this request, figuring, well, what's the worst that could happen?

In answer to this query, ladies and gentlemen: *It's Matt the Mutt!* Here he comes, fresh from fucking the daylights out of Sausage, who's still lying discombobulated but highly satisfied on my bed up on the third floor. Matt's come down all the flights of stairs in just a few seconds. He hits Mrs. Towson like an avalanche off the Matterhorn, and just like that Mrs. Towson is on her ass and the tray full of guacamole and chips is rotating through the air. As Hildegarde enters the room, Mrs. Towson, a lovely, round woman wearing a dress covered with large purple flowers, finds herself covered with guacamole and surrounded by pieces of broken dishes. There are corn chips on the floor, in her clothes, in her hair. Matt is lapping up the loose chips as if there's no tomorrow. Now he's lapping the guac out of Mrs. Towson's hair.

"No," says Hildegarde. "No!"

"Why, I—," says Mrs. Towson.

Hildegarde is pulling back on Matt's choke chain-collar and now he is coughing and hacking as if he's being strangulated. He snaps out of Hildegarde's hands and runs around the room. He gets as far as our freezer, in which an entire side of beef is stored in separate pieces individually wrapped in butcher paper, each one marked RIB EYE or GROUND BEEF or ROUND STEAK, and then he raises his leg and pees on the freezer. There's another knock on the door, and in comes Mrs. Larou, who lives just down Devon Boulevard. She has a plate full of deviled eggs. Matt looks over at her.

"No," says my mother. "Matthew! No!"

But Matt the Mutt will not be counseled. He sees Mrs. Larou, and her platter full of deviled eggs, and he knows what must be done.

Shortly before my sister boarded the plane for Minnesota, my parents had gathered us around the living room fireplace once more. It was not clear, during this period, if Dad's melanoma was in remission or what, and I feared, given their somber expressions, that they were going to tell us that Dad's cancer had indeed metastasized. Instead my father explained, in his quiet, twinkling, academic manner, that a socialist magazine in Minnesota had declared that he was one of the top ten people to kidnap in America. It was an honor, I guess, but not the kind you wanted.

Why anybody would want to kidnap my father is beyond me. Even if you believed that the world would be better off without capitalist stooges, surely there were better people to ransom than Dad. As far as capitalist stooges went, he was more Shemp than Curly. I'm not saying he wasn't a stooge, but please. He was a long way from Moe.

My guess is that the person who wrote the article hadn't really done much research. The writer had come up with this story in the same way that I, some years later, would come up with an explanation to a police officer for why I was driving a car wearing the bottom half of a gorilla suit. Dick Boylan was an innovator, to be sure, in the field of financial instruments, and no one would mistake him for Noam Chomsky. But all things considered, if what you wanted was to bring about a more just society, there were all sorts of other people you'd want to murder first.

My father thought the whole thing was funny—not the threat of being whacked, but the idea that anyone would think he was important enough to kidnap. The FBI, however, didn't share his sense of humor, and Dad wanted us to know that we were all going to be followed around by undercover agents in the months to come and that we should make sure, therefore, that at all times we were behaving in compliance with the laws of the United States.

(It is worth mentioning that, these many years later, I have written to the FBI and requested the confidential files pertaining to my father under the Freedom of Information Act and likewise googled my father's name along with other key words such as "assassinate," "kidnap," and "stooge." The FBI wrote me back to tell me they didn't have anything; the Google searches yielded exactly nothing. Which leads to the conclusion that either the FBI is lying to me now or my father was lying to me then. Or, even more likely: that over the years this story has become completely distorted in my memory so that

I have, once again, turned Something That Never Happened into Mythological Family Legend.)

My sister, however, says she saw her FBI agent all the time at Carleton. She'd see him, now and again, lurking outside the dorm or hanging out on the street near some college-town bar, smoking a cigarette. She and her friends would wave to him, and he'd nod back.

As for me, I never saw anyone, which makes me think that either the FBI suspected I was too inconsequential to kidnap or (more likely) I was so oblivious to everything that a federal agent followed me around for a year or so and I never noticed.

I know this story makes me sound slightly deranged, as though I am the transgender version of Chuck Barris, and that's a little embarrassing. On the other hand, I had drinks with my sister just a couple of months ago and I asked her, once again, about this business, and she affirmed that she'd been followed around all her freshman year at Carleton by a private dick, not to mention a whole bunch of fraternity boys.

Where was he, then, I ask, the day my sister was walking through the streets of Northfield, Minnesota, and encountered the adorable child pulling a wagon? Where was he when the child pointed to the tiny puppy in the wagon, an adorable white fluff ball with black patches over his eyes and ears? "You want a puppy?" said the child. "His name is Matthew."

My sister thought the situation over. She had a choice. On the one hand, she could keep on walking, maybe head up to the library, maybe work on a paper she had due. On the other hand, she could take the unspeakably adorable puppy into her arms, thank the child, and commence a new life as a dog owner. Matthew could live in her dorm room. She imagined, as hippies in a commune might raise a baby, that *they could all share him.* The dog was hopelessly, heartbreakingly cute. I ask you, who would *not* have taken the puppy?

Oh wait. I thought of someone.

My mother passed away in 2011, just shy of her ninety-fifth birthday, and if she were reading this today, at the crisp age of one hundred plus, I imagine she would even now clear her throat and raise one delicate, fragile hand.

Because of course, at the end of her freshman year, we will pick up my sister at the Philadelphia airport. We get her luggage off the baggage carousel, but then she says, "Wait, there's just one more thing."

"What?" says my mother, already fearing the worst. *"What?"*

A moment later, a crate pops down the conveyor belt, a crate that contains the adorable Matt the Mutt, who looks out upon this new world through the bars of his cage, upon the members of my family with an expression not unlike Aragorn as he makes his final entrance into Minas Tirith. *Rejoice, my people,* Matt suggests. *I have come to dwell among you all my days.*

Late in her life, Dodie Smith wrote a sequel to *The Hundred and One Dalmatians, The Starlight Barking.* In it, all the dogs in England awake to find their humans in a deep sleep from which they cannot be roused. Cruella de Vil makes a brief cameo, although she, too, is asleep. The dogs head to Trafalgar Square, where Sirius, Lord of the Dog Star, addresses all dogdom from the top of Nelson's Column. From this vantage point, he gives the dogs of the world a choice—to join him on the dog star, where they can all live forever in *bliss*; or to remain on Earth and take their chances with humanity.

Pongo—one of the heroes of *The Hundred and One Dalmatians*—takes a walk through the National Portrait Gallery in hopes of settling upon the right answer. He's especially moved by the plight of all the lost dogs, creatures who surely must feel that Sirius's offer is alluring.

"Today we have hardly felt like lost dogs," one says. "Because in a way, *all* dogs have been lost."

In the end, the dalmatians decide to remain on Earth. "Perhaps one day, Sirius," thinks Pongo, "we shall be ready to join you and accept bliss. But not yet."

Thanksgiving 1979. My grandmother, sitting in a green wing chair by the fireplace, rattles the ice cubes in her empty highball glass. "Voka," she says. My father takes her glass and heads out to the kitchen. In a love seat upholstered in white linen sit my grandmother's friend Mrs. Watson and my aunt Gertrude. Mrs. Watson has a hard time hearing anything, which sounds sad but actually works out for her pretty well. Aunt Gertrude is looking wistfully at the Cable-Nelson in the corner. "I wish I knew how to play the piano," she says. "I'd play it for you."

"You *do* know how to play the piano," says my mother. "You've been playing the piano since we were children!"

"Do I?" says Aunt Gertrude, always interested to learn things about herself.

"You don't remember *anything*!" shouts Gammie. "Hildy, get her something to drink."

My mother hates being called Hildy. "Can I get you anything?" she asks her sister.

"Maybe . . . ," said Aunt Gertrude, but then her sweet face is overcome with uncertainty and worry. She's overwhelmed by her choices. "Maybe some prune juice?"

My mother looks at me. "Jimmy, could you get your aunt some prune juice?"

"Sure," I say.

"And put some voka in it!" shouts Gammie.

"I don't want anything to drink!" says Aunt Gertrude, worried.

"How would you *know*?" asks Gammie.

"Jimmy, you're not going to put anything in my drink, are you? Promise me you won't!"

It hurts my feelings that Aunt Gertrude thinks I'd dose her, because I wouldn't. But my aunt has decided that I cannot be trusted. My mother leans forward and whispers in my ear, "Maybe you could just give her a little."

"You know what's interesting?" says Gammie, pulling her latex breast prosthesis out of her bra. "This looks *exactly* like a real boob!" She'd had a mastectomy the year before. We'd been worried about her, but Gammie now appeared to be perfectly okay. "Science is just something," she says. "That they could do this!" She waves the boob around. "Science!"

It is impressive—science, that is. "Here ya go," says Gammie. She hands the boob over to Mrs. Watson. "Maybe *you* could get one, Hilda."

"Whoop? Whoop?" says Mrs. Watson, which is her all-purpose response when she can't hear what's going on. When I was young I thought Hilda's deafness and her constant mantra of *Whoop? Whoop? Whoop?* was very funny. But now that I am old and have hearing aids myself, I've come to appreciate the utility of *Whoop? Whoop? Whoop?* It says what it means.

Hilda holds Gammie's breast prosthesis in her hands thoughtfully and considers the situation she's in. She was a World War I army nurse, widowed young. When she isn't going *Whoop? Whoop? Whoop?* she has a gentle Yorkshire accent. She has been my grandmother's best friend for decades. They used to live next door to each other when they both had apartments in the old John Wanamaker mansion on 2032 Walnut Street off Rittenhouse Square. This was the only house I was ever in that felt more haunted than the one my family had moved into. It was a crazy Jacobean Revival–style mansion, once owned by the department store magnate, that had since fallen on hard times. Once, my grandmother took me into the basement, which was stuffed with statues and old wedding dresses and steamer trunks. In one corner was an *actual stuffed fucking bear,* standing on its hind legs. The bear was dusty. "The people who owned this stuff are dead," my grandmother announced with a strange satisfaction. *"Dead!"*

"I'll be back," I say, taking Aunt Gertrude's glass and heading into the kitchen. My mother holds up her thumb and forefinger in the universal symbol for "just a little."

In the kitchen my father is sitting quietly at a table and smoking a cigarette. The round, claw-footed table is the same one at which six years earlier my friend John had looked around and noted that the *walls were breathing.* Gammie had found the table in the basement of the Wanamaker mansion. "Hey, old man," I say to him.

"Hey, old man."

My grandmother's empty vodka glass sits upon a table. "Mom wants me to put some vodka in Aunt Gertrude's prune juice," I observe.

He blows out some smoke. "Why not?" he asks.

"You want me to make the drink for Gammie, too?"

He nods. "You bet."

My father is wearing plaid pants and a blue oxford-cloth shirt monogrammed with his initials: JRB. Dad still smokes L&M Kings. My mother can't stand the fact that he smokes. But every time he tries to stop, he turns into an almost unrecognizably angry, short-tempered grouch, and rather than share a house with this irritable stranger, my mother has surrendered to the smoking.

Matt the Mutt sleeps upon the floor at my father's feet. It is rare to catch him in a moment of repose.

I mix up the drinks. After I nearly fill Aunt Gertrude's glass with prune juice, I look at it uncertainly. "You really think I should put alcohol in her drink?" My father is staring toward the ceiling, watching the smoke from his cigarette curl and dissipate. For a moment he doesn't respond. Then he looks at me, eyes shining.

"Do you miss her?" he asks me.

He's talking about my sister, who got married a year and a half ago, in between her junior and senior years at college, and who's since moved to Oregon, where she is teaching special-needs kids. In just a few months, Mount St. Helens will explode, leaving an inch of ashes all over her front yard. Cyndy will sweep some of these into an envelope and mail them to me in Connecticut, where by then I'll be living in a group house with a bunch of hippies in a comedy-group commune. As one does. I will hold the ashes in my hands and think of my sister all the way across the country.

I still have those ashes, still wrapped in a plastic bag inside a tin tea box that Gammie gave me when I was a child. I have a few old letters from Shannon in that box as well. The carnation I wore when I got married. A pregnancy stick with two lines in it. Some old love letters. A photograph of London Donna that I can't quite bring myself to throw away. Plus, the ashes of a volcano.

"Yeah, a little," I said.

My father nods. It's our first Thanksgiving without Cyndy, and everything feels a little weird. I am happy that my sister is in love and that she has found something—teaching—that she seems to enjoy so much, and I love that she is embarking upon a new adventure. But it hurts my feelings that my sister has launched upon a new life without me. The way I figure, I will never launch upon anything. Oregon is undiscovered country as far as I'm concerned. I've never been farther west than Ohio. My sister says she's seen the Pacific Ocean, a thing so vast I cannot possibly imagine it is real.

In the years since then, I have come to understand that this is exactly what happens: you get used to a certain way of being in the world, and then it changes. The people you love move away, or die, or something else happens—sometimes you just fall out of the habit of friendship, and the friend who you once saw almost every day becomes someone you track distantly—through Facebook, or Christmas cards, or not at all. I've had children of my own who've grown and moved away, and now I understand that feeling those pangs of distance and change is far more normal than any reliable routine. But in November 1979, this was all new territory. Sometimes the passage of time feels terribly personal, as if mortality is something they came up with just to hurt your feelings.

My sister had called us earlier that morning in a panic. She'd taken her turkey out of the refrigerator and found the giblets still frozen inside the cavity. Somehow she'd panicked and concluded that the turkey she'd bought from a farmer's market had not been properly dressed and that it would fall to her to do the ceremonial disemboweling. My mother had talked her down, finally convincing her that she just had to run a little hot water into the cavity to accelerate the melting process. Still, my mother had been unnerved by this call. Cyndy had seemed pretty upset, considering it was just giblets.

"I miss her, too," says my father.

I pick up the glasses with the prune juice and the vodka. "Guess I'll head back out," I say.

"Oh," says Dad. "Stay a little." He's not heading back into the fray until he's finished smoking his cigarette. I've never smoked, marijuana notwithstanding, but the look of satisfaction on my father's face as he blows the smoke from his L&M King into the air is compelling.

I sit down at the table next to him. "I'm glad you two . . . ," he says, and then, midsentence, sucks on his cigarette and holds in the smoke. This is one of my father's signature moves—getting half of a sentence out and then making you wait while he holds the smoke in his lungs—and it's either endearing or infuriating, depending. He blows out the smoke. "Became friends."

I nod. Taking an emotional inventory of things, as I noted earlier, is not exactly in my father's wheelhouse. "Yeah, well," I tell him. "We decided it would be more fun to gang up on you."

He chuckles in his twinkly way. "You know, we might have spent a little too much time . . . ," he says, and takes another big lungful of smoke and holds it in. I wait for him to exhale. As I wait, I hear Matt the Mutt, asleep at our feet, barking in his dreams.

"Following the horses," says Dad.

I don't really know what to tell him, because of course this is true. "It's fine," I say.

"You never cared too much for the horses," he says.

"Not really."

"I know. You found your own way, though." He nods, and his gaze becomes distant again. I have no idea what he's thinking about. Is it possible he is remembering the sound of Lloyd Goodyear, pulling his bow across his cello strings?

From upstairs, there comes a very slow, heavy sound. I know what this means, and I can suddenly foresee the future. Penny has jumped out of my bed on the third floor and even now is beginning the long, long voyage down the stairs toward the living room, where my mother and Hilda and Aunt Gertrude and my grandmother are still considering Gammie's latex breast. This is the world we live in. Jimmy Carter is president.

"I think it's very satisfying," my father says, "that you've done so much at Wesleyan." He chuckles quietly. "After they wait-listed you."

It's interesting that my father's mind has now alighted upon the injustice of my having wound up on the wait list at Wesleyan. I have continued my reign of terror as the overachieving child of the family, weird as I am, editing the college newspaper, winding up on the board of directors of the radio station, and by all measures acting as though I am *heavy business* at the college, and this gives my father great satisfaction after I was so nearly rejected. All in all, I am a good boy, the child my parents don't need to worry about, a status that will continue on for a few more years until my sister and I change places, and all at once she is the good child and I am the source of the unending heartbreak and scandal that rips us all apart.

Matt the Mutt raises his head suddenly. Up periscope. Penny is coming down the back stairs. A moment later, she arrives in the kitchen, and the future I imagined now comes to pass. Penny looks around with an expression that suggests, *Who are all these people? I seem to recognize them from somewhere.* Then her eyes alight on Matt and his upon her. Matt is up! He's on his feet! He gallops to her side! In a single swoop, he mounts the old dalmatian and he's in like Flynn! *Whoop! Whoop! Whoop!*

Penny, no longer a young dog by any measure, looks at the ceiling in rapture.

Remember the night we broke the windows in this old house? This is what I wished for, George Bailey.

My father stubs out his cigarette, and the two of us consider the fucking dogs. Matt the Mutt, incredibly, has been neutered, but you'd never know he was shooting blanks given the enthusiasm of his ministrations. Penny, for her part, is a changed woman since Matt came to town. In part this is because she was diagnosed with a thyroid condition and is now on medication that has restored the hair on her tail and also put an end to the flowing brown goo that oozed out of her eyes in days of yore. Penny, well into her eighties by now in dog years, is suddenly walking around on spotted paws singing, "Ah! Sweet mystery of life, at last I've found thee."

Matt finishes up, then turns to my father with a look that says, *Can't live with 'em! Can't live without 'em! Amiright?* Then he walks over to the wall, raises one leg, and pees on it.

"I got it," I say, and head over to the sink where a roll of paper towels and Top Job are permanently left out. I wipe up the puddle as Matt heads out of the room. Penny lies down, contented.

"That Matthew is a character," my father says in a voice that suggests he finds the dog's antics charming. This isn't all that surprising, as my father generally found everything charming, except when he was trying to quit smoking, when he generally found everything to be the opposite.

"What are we going to do about him?" I say.

Dad looks perplexed. "Do? What do you mean, do?"

"I mean," I say, "he pees in the house. He bounces all over everybody when we come in the door. He barks at you if you try to stop him from bouncing and peeing. He humps everything. He's kind of, you know, terrible."

Dad nods happily. "Penny seems satisfied."

"He was raised in a college dorm room! Then Cyndy just left him here! What are we going to do, just keep—living like this?"

My father seems confused by my passion, given that, technically, I don't live like this at all. Nine months of the year I'm off at college, and after my senior year it is my father's fond hope that I will head off to law school. Still, it infuriates me that the house my parents have spent years renovating smells like pee and that you can't walk in the front door without Matthew taking you down like a left tackle sacking a quarterback.

"What do you suggest?" my father says, giving me a look.

"I don't know," I say.

"We're not giving away your sister's dog," he says, and he makes it clear this is a matter of principle for him.

"Couldn't we take him to, like, dog-training school?"

My father smiles wanly at this, as if I have suggested that we might teach the dog how to operate a forklift. He looks at me adoringly, as if the fact that I would suggest something so completely out of the question is just testimony to the fundamental goodness and idealism of my character.

Through the door behind us is the entry room of the big old house, and in one corner of that room is the dog door that leads out to the kennel. A few months earlier—at the end of my junior year—I had come home from a semester in London. I'd thought, melodramatically, of never coming home, of just starting life over again in England as a different person. But I didn't know how to start life over. The things I wanted seemed impossible. Plus, I missed my family— Dick and Hildegarde. Gammie and Hilda. Aunt Gertrude. And my sister.

Penny and Matthew.

I'd traveled around Europe for a while after I finished up the semester in London. My friend Zero and I climbed a mountain in Spain and pitched a tent and ate baguettes and drank wine for a week or so. We walked around naked on the mountaintop. We kept milk cold in a small patch of snow. Below us was a vast valley, surrounded by rippling green mountains. One evening we watched a shepherd miles and miles away leading his flock home at sunset. The sound of tinkling bells around the goats' necks came to us across this inconceivable distance.

I'd finally taken my leave of Zero in Ireland and hitchhiked to Dún Laoghaire, taken the Sealink to Holyhead and a train to London, where I spent the long morning wandering the streets looking for a robe embroidered with a Chinese dragon I'd decided I wanted to buy for London Donna. (But the market where these things were sold was closed, and I just stood there looking mournfully at the shuttered bazaar.) Then I took a train to Heathrow, and a plane to New York, and then an Amtrak train to Philly, and then, at last, the local train back to Devon, where, at 1:00 A.M. on a summer night, I walked with my ridiculous backpack up the dark suburban streets of my adolescence. I arrived at my parents' house, just as I had left it. I was wrong when I thought I'd never come home. As it turned out, I'd keep returning to this house, again and again, until my fifties. My own children eventually came to call it "the mother ship," a place where it seemed, at one time, that my mother would live forever.

It was locked that night, though, and I knew that outside of waking up my parents, there was only one other option. So I put my backpack down and I went into the kennel and climbed the cinder-block staircase that led up to the dog door. And then I squeezed through it. I got stuck briefly, like the Grinch in the chimney. Matt the Mutt wandered into the back room. He didn't think it was unusual to see me wiggling through the dog door in the middle of the night. He began to lick my face, so violently I was afraid for a moment he might lick it off completely. I'd traveled halfway around the world, but now I was home.

With my sister's departure for the West Coast, I am suddenly the only person under the age of fifty in my family's circle. I understand that it is my job now to play the role of son, chauffeur of the elderly, changer of lightbulbs, mixer of drinks. It's not a role I'm particularly good at, and my sarcastic, narcissistic character makes my resentment of my responsibilities all too obvious. Still, I do the job anyway, not because I want to but because I have to. There are times, like now, when my father gives me a look, as if to remind me, *Taking care of other people is its own reward.*

It is a view of the world that I struggle to live up to. If I am honest about it, I'm still trying to live up to it.

From the living room comes a scream and then the sound of many raised female voices. Penny sits up and growls, the hair on her back standing up like a Mohawk. Matthew barks, and there's more screaming.

"Ah," says my father. "There we go."

We both get up and head into the living room. To get there we have to pass through the ornate blue dining room with its antique fireplace and a grandiose chandelier, through the entry hall with its sweeping oaken staircase, through a large arch with a keystone that leads into the formal room that contains the piano, and another fireplace, and my father's collection of rare first editions by Somerset Maugham, and the oil painting of my scowling grandfather, and my screaming relations.

Matt the Mutt is making the scene! He's got Hilda Watson's leg! He's humping her Yorkshire kneecaps! My mother is shouting, *No, bad dog, down!* and Aunt Gertrude is sniffing her prune juice for vodka, and Hilda, as the dog fucks her leg, is still holding my grandmother's latex breast, and Gammie is smoking a Parliament and laughing her head off, wearing an expression of delight, as if she had rubbed Aladdin's lamp and wished for just one thing, and this was it.

Penny enters the room and stands beside my father and me with an air of disappointment, like—*I let you out of my sight for one moment, and now you're seeing Hilda Watson's leg behind my back.*

Hilda's hands are up in the air, hallelujah style. She's still got the latex breast. *Whoop!* she says. *Whoop! Whoop!*

No, my mother says, now on her feet, tugging back on Matt's collar. But Matt is determined. Nothing can stop him from expressing his love for the leg of his dreams.

My father smiles gently, looking on. For just a moment his gaze falls upon the portrait of his father. *You shouldn't have left me,* he wants to tell old James Boylan, my grandfather. *You'd have found things so entertaining, if you had not died.*

A month later, I drove Matt the Mutt to the vet in my parents' car, a cream-colored Oldsmobile Omega. It's the same car in which I once kissed Shannon. I hadn't heard from her in a while, and now that I had, finally, been the object of someone's actual affections, I thought about her less. I had received lovely letters from London Donna the summer before. She signed them *Je t'aime* and drew hearts on the envelope.

Still, something in me had already been trained to think of myself as fundamentally undeserving of love, and in years to come when women would say *Je t'aime* or its equivalent, my first reaction was to think, *Yeah, well. That's only because you don't know me well enough.* It's a conviction that's hard to drop, once you get used to it, even after you've spent half your life (as I have) married to someone who makes clear every day exactly how much she adores you. In the twenty-first century, when I receive the sacrament of ashes, instead of saying, "Thou art dust" (the standard observation for the occasion), the pastor of Riverside Church will take me in her arms and say, "Jenny Boylan, you are beloved by God," and I will collapse in her arms like a rag doll, sobbing, so surprised am I, even after a lifetime of what turns out to be mostly joy, to be told that I am beloved by anybody. Even in my late fifties, when told by Reverend Doctor Amy Butler that I am beloved by God, my first thought is to protest—*That's just because He doesn't know me.*

But in this I suspect I am wrong.

Matt the Mutt, for his part, suffered from no such doubts. He was the canine version of Pepe Le Pew, or Donald Trump, convinced—all evidence to the contrary—that he was the most attractive and desirable soul on earth. Every time we yelled at him for peeing in the house, every time we yanked him by the choke chain off of yet another person's leg, he simply smiled at us with a look that said, *Zee leetle one, she is playing ze hard-to-get!*

I did not know what the vets had in store for Matt, although I suspected they had something. My mother had told me that the vets had "one more option" available for treating his exuberance and that I should tell them that it was time.

She didn't want to give me the details, but she said that the doctor would know what I meant.

Let us pause here for a moment, before we proceed on into the Tredyffrin/Easttown Veterinary Center, to deal with a little paperwork.

My sister, who had for a long time been absent from my life, and who then became the center of it, had now become absent from it once more, in part because she was now married and living on the West Coast and also because, of course, this is what happens in life: friends arrive, and then they disappear. We talked on the phone every week or so, and we also engaged in plenty of hilarious correspondence; I had a cartoon series called *Pigs on Motorcycles* that I sent her once a month that was, in its own way, a graphic continuation of the material I'd first explored as inventor of *The Hildegarde Time Show*.

But I'm suspecting that some readers—especially some of you who might have spent a little too much time reading books filled with clever jargon—might have been working up a little theory of your own regarding my adorable sister, namely, that the genesis of my transgender identity probably had something to do with my alternating jealousy of, and love for, her. If this thought has crossed your mind while reading this story thus far, then good for you! You're cleverer than this book's author by half and maybe should get into the authoring business yourself! You'd be surprised how enjoyable this new career might be! Plus, you get to travel around the world on airplanes and argue with right-wing pundits on television who will tell you, *I don't know you, Professor Boylan, but even without knowing you I can tell you I know you better than you know yourself!* Talk about fun!

Actually it is a theory more or less like this that my very first psychoanalyst will come up with in just a few short years. My reaction to this when he first reveals its brilliance will be a slight sense of confusion. Because sure: I loved my sister. How lucky was I to have someone in that haunted house with me when I was growing up who could *both* braid a pony's tail and play electric bass? But having her life? Please. I never wanted her life, not once. I mean, it was all right for her. But the life I wanted was my own.

I mention this because my shrink isn't the only person to come up with this theory, and to be honest, it feels more than a little insulting to me and a deliberate misunderstanding of what it means to be trans. When Shannon, decades later, learns that I am trans, she will also say something like *He always wanted to be me!*

I admired Shannon's brilliance as an actor, her sense of humor, her fierceness of character, and it's true that among the women I knew when I was young, she did provide a feminist model for how a woman could be in the world. There weren't a lot of women like that, at least not in Devon, Pennsylvania.

But I didn't want to be her, either. I'll hear this refrain again and again, after I come out and finally step into the world. The heartless and the cruel and the just plain stupid will declare, *Well, he just wanted to be like his sister, or his girlfriend, or little Natalie Wood,* and while I'm always delighted by the felicity of people's invention, the fact that such theories are colorful and clever should not overly distract us from the fact that they are, as it turns out, laughably untrue.

This is a good point to mention all this as well because in the story that lies just ahead I will find the first opportunity to leave the world of men in which I have dwelled. I was only nineteen or twenty, and to be honest, the boy who spent his days feeding Hamburger Helper to his Venus flytraps is not all that well buried within me, no matter how many letters I received from London Donnas declaring their love in French or how many evenings end with College Donnas imploring me to wait just long enough for them to get their birth control devices.

When I was young, I was haunted by the person I imagined I could never be. Now that I am old, what shocks me is not that, against all odds, I became that person. What shocks me now is that all the boys and men I once was still live within my heart, along with every last dog that ever helped them on their way.

The vet was out in Berwyn, which back then was a working-class town with a toilet seat store, a blacksmith, and a Mexican joint called Tippy's Tacos, where Jim Wilson and I had once engaged in a hot-sauce-eating contest that had not ended well. It was also the home of Conestoga High, where I'd have gone to school if my parents hadn't sent me to Haverford instead. The vet was close by a set of railroad tracks, where a year or two earlier a boy my age had been electrocuted on a signal bridge. I thought about him sometimes, wondered if he'd done it on purpose, wondered if that had solved anything, or if, like Anna Karenina, at the last second he'd thought, *No, wait, I've made a terrible mistake.*

"Come on, Matt," I said, pulling into the parking lot. The electric wires suspended above the Paoli Local tracks hummed in the early winter air. I put the dog on a leash, which he immediately began straining against. He yanked and bounced and jumped. "Just relax," I said to him, although given the mystery of the nuclear option I had come to explore, I can't say I'd have done much relaxing myself, were I the dog, which I was not.

We entered the vet's, checked in with the receptionist, who invited us to take a seat. It was just me and Matt in the waiting room, plus a guy who had what I presumed was a bird in a cage underneath a cloth. The cage was on the bench next to him. There were chirping sounds. Matt the Mutt bounced and yanked, like a jumping bean.

"He's a cute dog," the bird-man said.

I looked at Matt, the white fluff ball with the black spots on either side of his head. I had long since forgotten how adorable he was. "Yeah," I said. "He's pretty excitable, though."

The man nodded. "You have him fixed?" he asked.

I said yes. "He's still all wound up, though." Matt was desperately trying to get to the man's leg.

"I had a dog like that once," the man said. "Now I got a bird."

I looked at the cage, hidden by the sheet. "Is your bird sick?"

"Well," he said. "His droppings is all bloody."

"That's a shame," I said.

"Tell me about it."

The vet came out, and Matt and I were ushered in to a private examination chamber. "Ah, Matthew," he said. The vet was a young man, not much older than me. He wore a white coat with his name stitched into it in red thread. He looked good. I remembered how I had wanted to be a veterinarian when I was a child, but the prospect of med school was just too overwhelming. I wanted to help animals, but it seemed as if the only way to do this was through the terrible portals of organic chemistry and cell biology. *So,* I'd thought: *Forget that.* "What seems to be the problem?"

"He's really out of control," I said. "He humps everything, pees everywhere, knocks people over when they come through the door, stands there and barks at you if you try to tell him *no.*"

"And having him neutered hasn't changed any of this," said the doctor.

"No," I said. "He hasn't . . . slowed down at all."

"Hm," said the doctor. "Well, let's take a look."

The vet listened to Matt with a stethoscope as the dog squirmed and bounced. It was as if he were the dog equivalent of young Elvis.

After a while, the doc took the stethoscope out of his ears. "Well, there's nothing wrong with him," he said. "He just needs firmness, and training. He's developed some bad habits. You need to show him who's boss."

"My mother said you discussed . . . some other option?"

The vet thought about this for a moment, puzzled, then understanding broke through. "Ah," he said. "Well, there is one thing we can do. It's experimental. But we could give the dog hormones, you know, that would have a sedating effect. It's an experimental protocol."

I listened to the vet's words as if they were reaching me from a great distance. If I understood him correctly, what he was suggesting was we give Matthew female dog hormones. The theory being that a little estrogen might provide perspective.

This was a long time ago, and to be honest I can't remember the exact names of the drugs the vet had in mind, and in retrospect it seems insane, like something I must have dreamed. But a little research on the always reliable internet suggests that this is a course of treatment provided for aggressive male dogs, at least in some instances.

The drug the doctor had in mind was probably not diethylstilbestrol, although this particular compound was one that had crossed the Boylan family threshold once before. My mother had been given this drug, a synthetic hormone, during her pregnancy with me, in fact, since she was in her forties then and was considered to be at elevated risk for miscarriage.

DES was taken off the market in 1971, though, after scientists concluded that it caused cancer, and birth defects, and a host of other issues. One side effect of DES was an alleged increase in intersex and transsexual "conditions" for fetuses exposed to the drug in utero. I'm not especially swayed by this connection, and not only because the science is still inconclusive. I don't discount the effect of hormones upon our sense of self. But we are more than our chemicals, and surely some aspect of our souls comes from a place we cannot name.

"And would this be safe? For Matt, I mean?"

The doctor shrugged. "I wouldn't recommend it."

"What are the risks?"

"Well, you know," the doctor said. "You'd be *feminizing* your dog."

"I think my mother thinks he'd just calm down a little."

"Well, he might calm down," said the doctor. "But he wouldn't be—you know. The same dog."

All at once we were in the heart of a complex philosophical conversation.

"Is it dangerous?" This wasn't the question I really wanted to ask.

"Not dangerous exactly," the doctor said. "I just think there are better methods."

"Such as . . . ?"

"I think you should try to train your dog," he said. "You ought to work with him. Drugs are the easy way out."

I knew what he meant. But if I understood my mother correctly, the easy way out was exactly what we'd been looking for. Plus, what did it mean, that the dog would be feminized? So like, if we were driving in a car, Matt the Mutt would no longer be quite so reluctant to ask for directions? If we went to visit a friend, would Matt the Mutt henceforward insist that we *just bring our host a little present?*

"We can give you a sample if you want to give it a try," the doctor said.

"But you're saying you think it's a bad idea?"

"Like I said," the vet said. "You might not recognize your dog after."

I left the vet's with the pills in a canister. The man with the bird was gone.

On the way back to the house, Matt had his whole body out the passenger-side window of the Omega, his jowls and face blubbering in the air like an astronaut experiencing the incredible g-forces of lift-off. He stood there erect and joyful, the dog in full. He was like Sir Edmund Hillary atop Everest, like Neil Armstrong standing in the Sea of Tranquility. The winter sun shone down on his fluffy black-and-white face. Clouds of glory followed in his wake.

I pulled the car into the driveway, put Matt on the leash. In one hand I held a sample of feminizing hormones.

Dog hormones, to be sure. But hormones notwithstanding.

What would you have done, if you were me? Would you have maybe taken just one, to see what things might happen?

If you didn't like it, you could always just not take more. Call it an experiment that didn't work out.

If you did like it, well, there'd be more where that came from.

I know lots of transgender people who have their own version of the dog-hormone story, especially people who transitioned back when our very existence seemed debatable, before the scientific and political communities unanimously determined that people in such profound need should surely be helped and that the best response to this lifelong sense of wrongness is compassion and kindness.

Thank goodness everything has changed, and no one ever has to suffer through what I went through again. Ha! Ha! Ha! Ha! Ha! Ha! Ha! Ha! Ha! Ha! Ha! Ha! Ha! Ha! Ha! Ha! Ha!

I know a woman who stole her wife's birth control pills, took them on the sly. One of her breasts grew a lot, the other just a little. I know another woman who says that while riding a motorcycle, she was stung by a bee that "reset her endocrine system." I know others—lots of them, hundreds, in fact—who have ordered illegal hormones from Mexico off the internet, women who had silicone injections in their breasts that migrated unpleasantly throughout their bodies. Sometimes, in the wake of these choices, they died.

Then there is Candy Darling, of Warhol's Factory, who popped estrogen pills as if they were Good & Plenty. They gave her amazing skin, incredible breasts, and cancer.

I know thousands and thousands of transgender people who have tried to find their way in the unforgiving world—without resources, without support, without love. Is it really so surprising that anyone should rely upon their own cunning in order to outsmart a medical and therapeutic community that, for so long, sought only to deny us the treatment we so desperately needed?

You add everything up, filching hormones from the family dog doesn't seem like such a stretch.

As for me, the thing I didn't know was what would happen if, against all odds, I had my heart's desire. In the end, might I not be just like Gomer all those years ago—who did not know what to do with the thing he had always wanted (that is, my throat) when he finally got his paws upon it?

It wasn't that I didn't know who I was or what I wanted. But I was afraid.

Plus, there were times when being a boy—or a young man, as you'd have to call me by this point—was not without its pleasures. Sure, it was my second-best life. But my best life seemed to offer only violence and chaos. In the meantime: I'm the editor of *The Wesleyan Argus*. I'm trailed by girls who look at me with desire and call me Jaaames. I play Autoharp in coffeehouses where people are stunned by my little folk songs that manage to be both crazy funny and unbearably angry.

Like I said, there is something highly entertaining about "Imitation Imitation."

Perhaps one day, Sirius, we shall be ready to join you and accept bliss. But not yet.

On the way into the house I lifted the lid off the trash can and stuck the drugs in the garbage.

My mother was sitting at the kitchen table, the round one with the lion claws, when I came through the door. "Well?" she said. "What did the vet say?"

Penny wandered into the room, laid eyes on Matthew. Matt took a look at her and thought, in his Pepe Le Pew voice, *Ze little love bundle. She is looking for ze trysting place!* He rushed to Penny's side, and then—he climbed aboard! Matt was having his way! The world lay at his paws.

We looked at the two of them, going at it.

"He says that we should take him to dog school," I said. "He says we need to show him who's in charge."

Matt threw back his head and howled. *Ze game of love,* he noted, *is never called on account of darkness.*

It was pretty clear who was in charge. It was not me.

IV

Brown, 1985

On the contrary. I didn't think I looked this good.

The Pacific Ocean crashed on the rocks before me. I raised my hands to the ocean, like the victim of a stickup. Then I took off all my clothes, stepped into the sea, and dove beneath the waves. It was cold. Everything below the surface was dark.

I'd come to the seashore in Olympic National Park at the tail end of a cross-country road trip I'd taken with my friend Peter Frumkin. He'd welcomed me to New York City on Veterans Day two years earlier, the autumn after I graduated from Wesleyan. I got off the train at Penn Station and we headed to a bar in the East Village, the Grassroots

Tavern. There, over a couple of pints, Peter unfolded a giant map of Manhattan and, with a Sharpie, outlined exactly where it'd be safe to walk and where it would not. Then he gave me a subway token. "Good luck," he said. "You're going to need it!"

A couple of weeks later, he got mugged in one of the places he'd said was safe.

The next day, I got breakfast at the Waverly Coffee Shop in the Village. I gave the waitress my order, and then she gave me a look. It was Shannon.

She invited me to join her after she got off from work that night. Which I did. We walked around the piers on the Hudson and looked at the distant Statue of Liberty, which was green.

Later, I spent the night at her apartment way uptown.

In the morning, I found the super in the apartment next door to hers. It was for rent. Shannon paid for the deposit and also helped me find a roommate, a friend of hers named Charlie Kaufman, a young filmmaker.

Years later, of course, he'd make *Being John Malkovich*, and *Adaptation*, and *Eternal Sunshine of the Spotless Mind*. These, of course, would be works of genius. But back then, like me, he was just one more doofus.

I settled into our new apartment and got a job cleaning toilets in a bookstore. In my spare moments I worked on a novel, about a wizard who owns an enchanted waffle iron.

I tried freelancing, traveled around the city researching stories of the obscure and opaque. On one occasion, I spent an afternoon with the members of a *Titanic* disaster fan group in a bar. After a few rounds, they started to sing: "It was sad when that great ship went down."

I interviewed officials at Amtrak, trying to figure out why train whistles sound like train whistles. Why do they use a G-major sixth chord (GBDEG) on all the engines? Why, oh why?

No one would tell me.

A year or two went by. Charlie moved uptown with his girlfriend. Shannon—whom for the second time in my life I somehow failed to befriend—headed off to Paris. I hated that I could not reach her, after she'd so generously helped me find my very first harbor when, filled with terror, I had arrived in New York City to make my fortune. But whatever it was Shannon was looking for, it did not appear to be me.

I got an editor to read my novel about the enchanted waffle iron. "Somehow," she said, "it lacks an emotional center."

After two years, I'd had enough. That was when I headed west with Peter. On the way we stopped at places such as Vent Haven, the museum of retired ventriloquists' dummies in Kentucky, or the Corn Palace in South Dakota. It was fun, the big road trip. But it was also kind of like rowing a lifeboat away from the *Titanic*. I wondered what all those people in the disaster fan club were celebrating. Was it simply that they were not the ones who were dead?

We camped on the beach on the Olympic Peninsula for a few days, Peter and I. That was when I woke at dawn and walked naked into the sea. I dove beneath those dark waves, then staggered back out.

I sat down on the beach and stared at the ground, like a blob of malformed pink flotsam washed up by a storm. I put my clothes back on, but this didn't raise my spirits. It was all the same to me.

Then a voice called out to me. "Hey, you," he said. I turned around, and there was an Indian, a member of the Ozette tribe. He pointed overhead and said, "Look. There's an eagle. Do you see?"

I hadn't. But there it was, soaring over my head in wide circles.

"If you only look at the ground," the man said, "you'll never see the eagles." Then he laughed merrily, as if this were the funniest thing anyone had ever said. "You have to look at the sky!" he said.

I asked him what his job was, and he just smiled wanly. "I control the tides," he said.

I got back from the trip out West and called up this girl. I'd met her a few months earlier, when I was part of a group called Hoch P'Tui Theatre. We'd taken an early-morning tour of the Fulton Fish Market together back in June, on my birthday. Together we watched as fishmongers and journeymen unloaded their catch: lobsters, oysters, sea bass, mahogany clams. A big guy pretended to cut the head off of a turtle. Everybody in Hoch P'Tui Theatre screamed as the big guy laughed and wiped his hands on his bloodstained apron. But that turtle was okay.

I'd been thinking about Rachel, a little, during the road trip with Peter. Even now it still seemed possible that I might be somebody different, if only I were loved deeply enough. Rachel was a book editor at a university press, a person who seemed so much like a grown-up I just assumed I'd never have a shot.

"I was hoping you would call," she said.

A few days later, Rachel came over to my apartment, one floor above an S&M dungeon. I played her some ironic coal-mining songs on my Autoharp.

Later, we walked out into the New York night, ate some dinner at a Chinese place on Broadway. Afterward we sat on a bench overlooking Riverside Park, in front of the very building that I would live in, forty years in the future. The skies grew dark, and it began to softly rain.

I put my arm around her, and we kissed. We thought about going back inside, what with the storm, but instead we just sat there a little longer, she and I, feeling the rain upon our faces.

———

By Thanksgiving we were living together. I wrote her a waltz on the piano. One of the verses went like this:

> *You are the smile of a cake on Bastille Day,*
> *A boat on a lake on the first day of June,*
> *You are the sun on a plate full of muffins,*
> *A flag at half-mast by a farm on the moon.*
> *You are the time on a watch with a broken chime.*
> *Here is a song you can sing in the bathtub,*
> *Here is a song when you're steeping your tea.*
> *Here is a song that is dumb but it's pretty.*
> *The song that the Halcyon sings by the sea.*

Not long after that we were walking from Peter's house on Washington Place back toward the Christopher Street subway station when suddenly, there on the street before us, was a young person with a box full of puppies. They were baby bloodhounds—wrinkly and floppy and adorable. I stood there on the street, my heart melting in two. *They were giving puppies away for free.* Rachel just looked at me and rolled her eyes. "What?" I said.

She pulled on my arm, and we headed toward the number 1 line. "I don't know," said Rachel. "I just don't really like dogs much."

One night, the phone rang. It was my mother on the line. "Jim," she said, "I'm sorry to tell you this, but we had Penny put down today."

The connection wasn't very good. There was lots of crackling static. "Put down?" I said. "What do you mean, put down?"

"She wasn't enjoying life," my mother explained.

"Oh, Penny," I said. "Poor Penny."

"I'm sorry," said Mom.

I hung up and sat there. Rachel hadn't met my parents yet. I was twenty-five years old. Whispering Winds had gone out of business a long time ago.

"What is it, James?" Rachel asked. "What's happened?"

I opened my mouth, but nothing came out. Tears spilled over my lashes, and a great gurgling sob erupted from me. I wasn't much given to crying, at least not in those days, but I was crying now.

After a while I tried to tell Rachel the whole story. There'd been this puppy I'd loved when I was eleven, but in time I'd turned my back on her, thrown my dog and her goo-oozing eyes out of bed because her gelatinous sadness was a merciless chain tying me to the person I no longer wished to be. I tried to explain all this, but I didn't get far. It wasn't just Penny that had been put down.

Rachel, who smoked a pipe, took the pipe out of her mouth and looked at me thoughtfully. "I'm sorry you're sad," she said.

It's funny how there really are dog people and cat people. Dog people are supposed to be more outgoing and loyal; cat people are supposed to be more creative and independent. For folks committed to a binary way of looking at the world, it can be entertaining enough to think like this.

I'm a dog person, obviously enough, but I've owned a few cats, too, and not just *Ba-boing!* When I was a child we had a cat named Sneakers who lived almost exclusively on birds and mice she caught in Earle's Woods. She'd disappear for weeks at a time, then show up at the house with a fat belly and a disturbing, satisfied expression. Then, when I was in college, I'd adopted a feral cat with big creepy thumbs for a few weeks. She proceeded to tear apart my dorm room and piss on my down coat, until finally, her work complete, she disappeared. I missed that cat after she headed out, but I got over it. I figured there was someplace else she needed to be. Cats are like that—they're not real good about sharing their plans, which I respect.

If you want to keep a secret, tell a cat.

Parsing the differences between cat people and dog people is fun, I guess, and why not: it's interesting to recognize our own truths reflected back at us in the behavior of animals.

But I admit I'm more interested in what becomes of dog people without dogs, or cat people without cats, or anyone who finds herself living a life in which something essential to her character is torn away from her. What happens to a husband, or a wife, whose life has been defined by the love they've shared, who then is suddenly alone—widowed, or separated, or abandoned for someone else? What happens to a father, or a mother, sundered from their child?

Of course, parents always lose their children, one way or another, and even if you are lucky enough to see them graduate from high school, or college, at some point they spread their wings. Then you wind up like me at age fifty-five, a mother wandering through the house looking at their fencing trophies and their old soccer balls, thinking: *Who am I, now that my child is gone? Surely after all these years, I am not no one?*

But I don't know. Was I so unlike a transgender person, who never finds the courage to come out? Was I so unlike a dog person, in love with a person who does not love dogs?

Rachel and I lived in my scary apartment above the S&M dungeon for a while, then moved to the East Side, into an apartment across from a city block where they were building a giant mosque with an ornate minaret. In my mid-twenties I got a job at Viking Penguin, working as a copy editor and an assistant to the managing editor, which is really kind of curious, given the fact that I could not spell. Still, I had a job with a desk and a telephone that had little blinking lights at the bottom and a little red button marked HOLD.

Sometimes I thought about telling Rachel about the thing that was in my heart, but then I wondered what end this would serve.

I would ride the subway to the Viking Press, then located about half a block from the Flatiron Building. In one hand I held a metal lunch pail, to which I'd affixed the Viking colophon—a single-masted ship with a square sail, a dozen sailors beneath it, bearing spears and oars. Speed lines radiating from the ship indicated that it was an object of light and illumination.

Inside the lunch bucket I packed turkey sandwiches and a banana, a thermos containing chocolate milk. I had a Ring Ding Jr. Sometimes Rachel wrote a note in pen on my paper napkin: *Have a nice day! I love you!*

Sometimes, on my way home, I'd stop off at a bodega and buy her a bouquet of flowers.

If you didn't look too closely, I might have seemed like a person beginning the days of her manhood. At the time I felt less like a man than someone imitating one—but then, people of transgender experience are hardly the only ones who suffer from this regret.

I'd look around our apartment, with Rachel's Vermeer painting and the books on the shelves and the big desk upon which I'd placed my very first computer—a Kaypro 2X—and think: *I am not nothing.* Surely this is the life I was hoping for, back when I was young and tried to imagine what it might be like, someday, to leave my dogs behind?

———

Then, one day in 1984, my father called me up and asked me if I'd pick up this new puppy they were getting, a chocolate Lab.

"Wait, what? You're getting another dog?" Penny and Matthew had both gone to their rewards by now, and it was my understanding that now that their children had flown, my parents were at last going to enjoy some dog-free years. This seemed like something that my mother, in particular, had yearned for, having spent most of the sixties and all of the seventies picking up dog shit with a shovel—or worse, given that Matt the Mutt rarely felt it necessary to bother with some of the formalities of relieving himself outside.

"You bet," said my father in his gentle, understated, crinkly fashion. He explained that the puppies had been sired by the dog of a business colleague of his and that they needed someone to rent a car, drive out to Montauk, and pick up the puppy and drive it to Pennsylvania.

"I can't believe you're getting another dog," I said, not only stunned that my mother had signed on for more dog ownership but a little bit resentful that my parents thought anyone could ever take the place of Sausage. "Are you sure this is what you want?"

"Why not?" said my father.

A week later, I was driving toward home with a puppy asleep in my lap, an adorable brown fluff ball that as yet had no name. The car filled with her wonderful puppy smell.

It occurred to me, as I crossed the Delaware River and saw the big sign—NOW ENTERING PENNSYLVANIA, THE KEYSTONE STATE—that I was doing the very thing for which dogs are celebrated: finding my unlikely way home, over a tremendous distance.

There is no shortage of stories of dogs, sundered from their loved ones, finding their way home after traveling hundreds of miles. The all-time record holder appears to be a Lab/boxer mix named Jimpa, who got separated from his master while he was working on a construction job in Western Australia. A year later, Jimpa showed up at his house, somehow having traveled two thousand miles to be with the one he loved.

It's not entirely clear how dogs do this, although surely their amazing sense of smell has something to do with it—dogs having many, many more olfactory cells than humans. Other research suggests it might also have something to do with sensitivity to magnetic orientation. One study cited in *The New York Times* shows that dogs will usually defecate in a north–south position, although this preference vanishes if the magnetic field is disturbed.

When my family moved into our haunted house back in 1972, we were surprised, several days after the move, to find a German shepherd lying beneath the apple tree in our backyard. My father, always ready to admit another dog into the house, called out to the shepherd, opening wide the back door to let him in. For the next half hour or so, the dog wandered around the house, as if looking for something he could not quite find.

The object of his search was no mystery: clearly the dog belonged to the Hunts (the house's previous owners), who'd let him out the door of their new home ten miles away, only to have him make the long trek back to the place where he'd lived before. It wasn't just the home he was searching for, either: it was the father of the family, who'd died a year earlier and whose loss had set the long process in motion that had ended with the Hunt family moving out and the Boylan family moving in.

We called up the Hunts and told them we had their dog. When

one of their sons showed up to claim him, he explained another possible reason for the journey. They'd had many shepherds over the years, he said, and all of them were buried in the backyard, beneath that big apple tree. Their dog had a habit of lying there, as if considering the road ahead.

My own journey back to my parents' house was a lot less unlikely than the journey of that shepherd or of Jimpa. But it felt no less miraculous to me, to show up at the back door of the home I'd grown up in. I'd stood by the Pacific Ocean and watched an eagle half a continent away. I'd hung out with the members of the *Titanic* disaster fan club. I'd made out with Rachel in the rain.

I'd had all those adventures, but I'd been drawn back home with a single twitch upon the thread. And there was my father, opening the door to let me in.

"Hey, old man," he said, looking at the puppy in my arms. "What do we have here?"

"I got the puppy, Dad," I said, and as I said it, something in my throat caught.

Did I know even then what was coming, the result of my unconscious attunement to a disturbance in the magnetic field?

He picked up the brown fluff ball, and his face crinkled and shone like the sun. "Who's a good girl?" he said.

We walked into the living room, my father and the new pup and I. There they were—my mother, Aunt Gertrude, Gammie, and Hilda, just as I had left them centuries before. They sat before the fireplace, under the watchful gaze of my grandfather. You could tell from his expression he was getting fed up with the bunch of us.

And there was my sister, back from Oregon. Cyndy put her arms around me. "Hey, little brother," she said, and kissed me on the cheek.

My grandmother rattled the ice in her glass. "Voka," she said.

My father passed the puppy to my sister and went out to refresh my grandmother's drink. Cyndy and I stood there beaming, breathing in the redolent puppy smell. "You know," she said to me, "I think that maybe, just once, we might have a dog that is not insane."

It occurred to me that she was right about our dogs—all of them thus far had been deranged, although each in a different fashion. I wondered, in passing, why this was true, but then at that same moment, Gammie pulled her breast prosthesis out of her bra again and started waving it around as she cackled with laughter. "Hey, Hilda," she inquired, "ever seen one of *these*?"

The question of why our dogs had always turned out to be mental was one that, really, seemed to answer itself. I looked at the adorable brown puppy in my sister's arms and hoped that this time our dog would turn out to be a civilized member of the family of nations. It was something to wish for, anyhow.

But it was early yet.

Rachel, of course, had not accompanied me on the journey to Montauk to get the puppy from the farm, nor had she joined me on the journey back to Devon. The morning after, however, she called me on the phone, asked me if I wanted her to come visit. I said I wasn't sure. She said there were two trains—she could arrive at 9:00 A.M. or at 11:00.

I talked to her as I sat in the living room, the chocolate fur ball in my lap. I said, "Well, either one is fine. Whichever one you want to take is great. I'll be waiting."

"Yes," said she. "But tell me which one is better."

"Well, if it's all the same to you," I said, "maybe the eleven o'clock one. That way I can sleep in."

There was a moment's silence. "Are you saying you don't want me to come?" asked Rachel.

"No, no," I said. "Take whichever train you want. I'm just saying. Since you asked. If you arrive at eleven, I won't have to get up so early."

"Well, I'd hate to disturb your sleep," said Rachel.

"Well, take the nine o'clock," I said. "That's fine."

"No, no," said Rachel. "I hate to be an inconvenience. Why don't I check the schedule again, there's probably one that arrives in the afternoon."

"Rachel," I said. "Please. Come whenever you want. I can't wait to see you." I ran my fingers against the dog's soft ears.

"It doesn't sound like it!" said Rachel. "It sounds like you don't want me to come at all!"

"Take the nine o'clock train!" I shouted. "Come at dawn! If there's a train at three A.M., take that one! I don't care!"

"I'm not coming!" she shouted.

"Fine!"

"Fine!"

We hung up. Brown raised her head and looked at me. *What*, she said.

Rachel called back an hour later. She'd booked the eleven o'clock train. I begged her to change it, to come earlier. She asked me did I *really* want her to come early. I said I really, really, really did.

And so on.

One night, I made Rachel the following dinner: fried chicken, served on a Belgian waffle, with a gelatinous brown sauce slathered on top. I called her to the table.

"James," she asked uncertainly, "what *is* this?"

It was a good question.

We had started fighting: a little at first, then a lot. I had never really been in a real relationship before, so I had no idea how to negotiate disagreement. Every parting of the minds struck me as the end of the world. I didn't know anything about the ways that couples compromised or tried to make their peace in the face of conflict. More seriously, I had no way of knowing when a relationship was not healthy.

I did not know what would happen to me if I broke up with Rachel or if, as the saying goes, *I sent my relationship to a farm*. I had longed my whole life to be this kind of man—someone with a serious job, someone who had given himself as completely to his lover as Dick Boylan had given himself to Hildegarde. I had long believed that if I could only invent this kind of life, the kind that all those boys I had grown up with seemed to inhabit, then I, too, could be like them and exist as something solid and opaque.

I wanted to be for Rachel what my father was for my family—the man who stood between the people he loved and the forces of chaos. If I lacked the certainty that was necessary to really protect her, I would, at the very least, try to *imitate* a man who had that sense of certainty.

I figured being a man was just something that I'd get better at over time, like playing the piano or fighting with a sword. I wasn't much of a sword fighter, but I thought I might improve, if I only got enough practice.

————

My sister and my father were crazy about the movie *Amadeus,* which was popular at the time, and for some reason my sister fell in love with the name of Mozart's wife, Constanze. In the movie, Wolfie calls her Stanzi, and it was this name that Cyndy convinced my parents to give the new dog.

It's adorable enough if you're Austrian, I guess. I thought it was terrible.

"Well, what do you think we should call her?" my sister asked me, annoyed.

"What would happen," I asked, "if we called the dog 'Nothing'?"

"The dog has to have a name!" my sister said, exhausted with me.

"No," I clarified. "The dog would have a name. But its *name* would be Nothing."

My sister gave me a look. "What's wrong with you?" she asked.

In the end the dog was just called Brown, a name that seemed to make up in truth what it lacked in imagination.

I've noticed this lots of times, that people come up with a grandiose name for their dog, or child, only to shorten it to something more practical over time.

In our family, actually, the second name wasn't always the more practical one. I can't remember what *Ba-Boing!*'s name was originally, but I can assure you it wasn't *Ba-Boing!* Penny, in turn, had become Sausage. Matt the Mutt, as I understand, also had a nickname during the time he lived in my sister's dormitory at Carleton, a name that is so obscene I cannot bring myself to type it out here, but which was a fairly accurate description of the way the dog liked to spend his free moments. Alex, the dog I adopted in my thirties, would also be known as Snedley; Ranger, many years later, was sometimes called Rufus.

I heard a story once about a set of new buildings that went up on a college campus, and instead of paving sidewalks right away to these new structures, the college waited for a year to see where the paths emerged, based on where students and teachers actually walked. Only after the paths of choice became clear did the college put in the sidewalks. It was in just this way that Stanzi became Brown.

Or that I, at age forty, would become Jenny.

Or that our child Zach, many years later, would tell his mother and me that he, too, was not whom we had thought.

My mother called me on the phone. There were some issues with Brown.

"Well," Mom said. "It's her paws. She kind of chews them, you see."

"She chews her own paws?"

"My dog book says it's called a 'lick granuloma.'"

I'd seen dogs who had this problem before, of course, dogs who start in on their paws and wind up obsessed and deranged, as if their paws are the dog equivalent of right-wing talk radio.

"She just chews them and chews them," my mother said, "creates these giant sores, and you know, well, they just bleed all the time, and then she chews them some more. It's like the dog wants to disappear. By swallowing herself, starting with her paws."

"Mom, you need to take the dog to the vet."

The vet, interestingly, was now a young man named St. George Hunt. He was one of the Hunt boys who had grown up in our house. (His older brother Al Hunt became a beloved journalist as well and was someone I would eventually cross paths with in Washington, D.C., while he was working for Bloomberg News.) As a child St. George had lived, for a while, in the room across the hall from the one I would live in in the 1970s, and—as he later explained it—one night some wandering spirit had encouraged him to jump out the window. He'd got one leg out the window when his father, hearing the commotion, hauled him back inside. Years later, I asked him if he would spend a night alone in the haunted house now. "Not for any reason," he said kindly. "Not for any price."

"Well," my mother asked, "could you come down from New York and help me get the dog to St. George? I can't take care of everything. I just can't anymore!"

"Is everything okay, Mom?" I asked.

She didn't answer right away. Instead, she started breathing funny, inhaling in little gasps. It took me a moment to realize that this was the sound of my mother crying.

I hadn't heard this sound very often, over the course of my young life. I had the strong suspicion that, whatever she was crying about, it wasn't the dog.

"Mom?"

I went down to Devon, spent a long weekend with my parents. My father sat by the fire, smoking a cigarette, drinking his Old Grand-Dad. He'd gotten his first blast of chemo already.

"How are you doing, old man?" I asked him. "Feeling okay?"

"You bet," he said, and blew the smoke toward the fire.

That Sunday my mother and I went to her little Lutheran church in Devon. She'd started going to church again after my father's cancer came back. On one wall hung a copy of a famous painting of Christ in Gethsemane. I remembered it from when I was a child, the frightening greenish Jesus looking up into a dark sky, wearing an expression that says, *Don't make me do it.*

I sat in the pew next to my mother that Sunday, listening to the pastor read from scripture. *Whoever lives in love lives in God, and God in him.*

What would it mean, I wondered, to be a person who belonged to God—whatever that might mean—and yet to never know God or to know that love? Would it be anything like the world I lived in now, a dog lover living in a world without a dog? Would it be anything like the life of a son who loved his father, whose father was taken away?

We got back from church to find my father reading a book of medieval history by the fireplace: *A Distant Mirror,* by Barbara Tuchman. In one hand he held his L&M King. Brown lay on the floor beside him, a cone of shame wrapped around her neck.

Now and again the dog would attempt to get at her elusive, delicious paws. But she couldn't reach them.

In the summer of 1985 John Barth, the novelist and critic, called me on the phone. I picked it up and stood there in the tiny East Side apartment I shared with Rachel. It had exposed brick on one wall, upon which hung the portrait of the *Girl with a Pearl Earring.* Now and again that woman would look at me with the same look that I had once seen on the face of Gomer the German shepherd. *I know who you are,* she said, although she said it in Dutch. Other times, she looked at me and just said, *Klootzak!*

Which is Dutch, more or less, for *Asshole!*

"Yes," said John Barth. "I wanted to tell you that you've been accepted for the graduate program at Johns Hopkins. We were all impressed with the felicity of your invention."

That girl in the Vermeer just rolled her eyes. *Klootzak!* she said, although I did not know if she meant John Barth or me.

"Well, thank you, Professor Barth," I said as the truth sank in. I'd been accepted to grad school! Me, the lunkhead!

"Jack," he said.

After I'd been accepted to graduate school, but before the semester actually began, I had a long, strange summer in which I knew that the world I lived in was shortly to disappear. I felt like a scuba diver running out of air. I quit my job at Viking after it was brought to my attention that many of the books I was working on were "riddled with errors," although in my defense I would like to note that those errors had their genesis with those books' authors and not with me. Still, some of the allure of parsing the difference between *mantel* and *mantle* (for instance) had begun to wane. Instead, I took on a series of temp jobs. In the mid-1980s, I was what was then referred to as a "word processor," a vocation for which I was particularly well suited, given my ability to type nearly one hundred words a minute. One day I worked for an imperious man in a Park Avenue tower who, upon my arrival, looked me up and down and then stated, "You're a man?" He sounded disappointed; he'd wanted to get me to make him coffee, but now he wasn't so sure.

I wanted to tell him, *Dude, you don't know the half of it.*

At a company called Schlumberger I worked on the oil trading floor, sending telexes, which was, in the summer of 1985, the high-tech version of instant communications. I spent all day sending telexes to Venezuela, where No. 2 fuel oil was pumped onto tankers. They had a particular way they wanted you to answer the phone there—you had to say your name and your department. Thus, I also spent some time responding to a bell that demanded I then say, in a clear, calm voice: "This is James Boylan, in oil."

Rachel and I trudged through that summer. She wanted to talk about ways of sustaining our long-distance relationship in the year to come. I held up my end of this conversation, but the fact of the matter was that I was sneaking off to Baltimore at least in part because it felt like a not dishonorable way of getting out of the relationship without having to actually break up.

I didn't know the first thing about how to end a relationship. Where would you learn such a thing? My dogs had always stayed with me, even Penny, whom I had done my best, in her declining years, to ignore.

One day I was temping at a company called Dun & Bradstreet. My mother reached me, somehow, and told me that my father was starting a new drug called vinblastine.

"He's going to be all right," I said to her. "Isn't he?"

A few weeks later Rachel left on a business trip—the American Historical Association, I think. I would be alone for three days. I knew that *On the Waterfront* was going to be on television that night, and I imagined getting Chinese takeout and a six of Beck's beer and watching Marlon Brando get beaten up. *I coulda been a contender.*

I was working for the *New York Post* at the time, and as I left work that day, I stepped into an elevator that contained Rupert Murdoch, all alone, and the two of us descended in silence. The doors opened, and we headed out into our respective worlds—Rupert to his, I to mine. People rushed around me as I wandered aimlessly across Manhattan. I walked more and more slowly until at last I stopped in front of the Empire State Building.

There was a shop on the first floor that sold wigs. I stared at all that hair, perched atop featureless Styrofoam heads. I looked east and west. I saw no one I knew.

There was a bell on the back of the door. It went: *Ding.*

Everything I know about love I learned from dogs.

From Playboy I learned that it is perfectly fine if everyone hates you as long as you are deeply loved by one person. And that sometimes what we are loved for is not our gifts but our faults.

From Penny I learned that sometimes love fades, that it can be hard to keep a promise at one age that you made when you were younger. I learned the terrible truth that as we morph from self to self over time, the love that one self has sworn can seem unfathomable to another.

From Matt the Mutt I learned that sometimes the happiest people are the ones that cause the most pain to everyone around them.

And from Brown I learned that sometimes those who appear the most normal are the ones who are craziest.

I had tried to be the gentleman's equivalent of Brown during my chocolate Lab days in New York. I wore a tie each day and rode the subway with my lunch bucket affixed with the Viking colophon, and I returned home in the evening and made chicken and waffles with gelatinous brown sauce for the woman that I loved.

But the second she turned her back I was slipping into a wig store in midtown. *Ding.*

Rachel was a strong, smart, and kind person, and it makes me feel bad that I was such a failure as a boyfriend to her, given how much she loved me. It wasn't her fault that I'd decided that I could not be myself with her. But then, if I'd shared my heart with Rachel, what would she have said?

When we visited my parents' house, I would read her the comics in *The Philadelphia Inquirer* in the mornings, just as my father had once read the funnies to me. I loved *Peanuts*, and owned several collections of the strips. One weekend, as I read *Peanuts* to her, it occurred to me that *Peanuts* was a universe of broken hearts: Charlie Brown loves the Little Red-Haired Girl, whom we never see. Charlie Brown's little sister, Sally, is in love with Linus, whose affections, in turn, are reserved for his blanket. Lucy is in love with Schroeder, but Schroeder is in love with Beethoven. Marcie is in love with Charlie Brown, and with Peppermint Patty, but Peppermint Patty loves only Charlie Brown. And so on.

There was one strip in which Violet tried to humiliate Pigpen. "Aren't you ashamed?" she says after making him look in the mirror.

"On the contrary," he replies. "I didn't think I looked this good."

Sometimes, in the mornings, I lay listening to Rachel's tender breath taken in sleep. I pictured myself knocking on her door *en femme,* her startled expression as she realized that the strange woman before her was someone she already knew. I imagined her response: *Aren't you ashamed of yourself?* Surely she'd want to give me a good scrubbing.

On the contrary, I might reply. *I didn't think I looked this good.*

By the fall I would find myself in Baltimore, sitting on a couch with an Irish writer named Jean, listening to a piano piece by Mussorgsky, *Pictures at an Exhibition.*

During a movement called "Catacombs," the music grew dark. I looked over at Jean, and she looked at me, and at that moment we came to an unspoken agreement about the trouble we were about to cause.

In the weeks to come, I would take care to wash my sheets. Jean had a cat, and Rachel was allergic. If Rachel came to visit me, she would realize something was up the first time that she sneezed.

For what reason, one might wonder, did Brown chew her paws? Was Brown, in the end, not so unlike me, driven to the ends of the earth simply because she could not quite do the thing that she was destined to do?

In Brown's case, this was swimming. As a Lab, of course, she'd been bred to spend her time in the water, and whenever she could she'd escape from my parents' house and dive into their ancient, leaking swimming pool, where she'd swim in circles for hours if given the chance, dog-paddling through those chlorinated waters with an expression of limitless dog joy.

My mother didn't like the idea of the dog in the pool, not only because of her theory that the dog hair got in the filter but also because, having lived through the Depression, there seemed something fundamentally wasteful about having a swimming pool for a dog.

My mother did her best to keep Brown inside, but even so, the dog found her way to running water. Using her snout as a forklift, she would shove a kitchen chair over to the kitchen sink, climb on top of the chair, and somehow get the spigot going with her teeth. There the dog would stand, for hours if no one was home, biting and snapping at the running water as if, even now, she might thus fulfill her genetic destiny.

Or, if my mother was so foolish as to run the sprinkler on her lawn, Brown would burst outside in order to cavort in the dancing waters. We would lock the doors and windows in order to prevent this. Brown, frustrated, just looked through the glass, watching the sprinkler soak the earth with an expression of longing.

It would be easy enough to explain all of this by saying the obvious:

Brown was a water dog, and what she wanted was water. It didn't seem like such an unreasonable demand.

One night, as the family gathered around the fireplace, someone noticed that the dog was missing. By the time we got out to the pool, Brown must have been swimming and biting the water for four or five hours. She'd swallowed so much water, in fact, that she developed a condition called "gastric torsion," or twisted stomach, as we learned when we hauled the dog off to St. George's vet clinic that night and he explained that her constant swimming and swallowing had now placed her life in danger.

He performed surgery on the dog to address this condition, but we were warned that henceforward, if we valued the dog's life, we had to keep her out of the pool. The twisted stomach had been resolved for now. But it might come back.

At about this same moment in my life, a friend of mine from high school became a heroin addict. Later, he explained to me how he'd gone to see his ex-wife one time, to beg her forgiveness for ruining their marriage with his addiction. She forgave him, he said, in a tearful scene full of forgiveness and loss. On his way out of her house, he stopped off in the bathroom. Where, his spirits having been raised by the sense of solace he'd achieved from the reconciliation, he shot up some more heroin.

He knew it was killing him. But sometimes a desire becomes so deeply ingrained in us that we don't know who we are without it.

My mother took to duct-taping the kitchen faucet handles when she was out, so the dog couldn't work her way over to the sink. But sometimes she'd come home to find that the dog had chewed her way through the tape.

I'm sorry, Brown seemed to say. *All I want in the world is the thing I know is bad.*

I cheated on Rachel within weeks of arriving at Johns Hopkins. My first transgression was with Jean, as we listened to Mussorgsky. Later, I cheated on Jean with Sandrine, whom I took out to dinner at a fancy restaurant called the Brass Elephant. Then I cheated on Sandrine with Samantha, a girl whom I first met as she was swallowing goldfish at a frat party. Later, she got sick, and the goldfish emerged once more, in an unpleasant inversion of the legend of Jonah and the whale.

I think one reason I had all these serial affairs was that the moment a woman got close to me, I realized that I had to either tell her the truth about my bifurcated soul or else just have a relationship based on a lie. I'd noodle around with these women, open myself up to them a little bit—but then the moment my private world felt threatened I'd have to disappear. Ghosting, I believe we call it now.

There was one woman who got through to me, though, a poet named Nancy Johnson. She was older than me by about a dozen years, which probably explained her uncanny patience with my cryptic antics. Nancy called me "Water Strider," in part because of my long, spindly legs and in part because of my elusiveness, but most of all because she perceived, somehow, that I was suspended between two worlds, in a manner not unreminiscent of the way a water strider balances atop the surface tension of the waters in a marsh.

She was at the tail end of a bad marriage then, and in my awkward way I tried to help her through those days of bereavement; they were not so unlike my own. My relationship with Rachel was clearly circling the drain. One night we listened to Dylan's "Tangled Up in Blue," and when our man sang the line about his lover being married when they first met—soon to be divorced—we both looked at each other with matching expressions of horror and recognition.

I sang tunes for Nancy on the Autoharp, songs I remembered from childhood as well as my own opaque ballads that hinted at—but never quite revealed—the thing that was in my heart. In the mornings when we rose, I would brush her long blond hair for her and bring her toast and marmalade on a plate. She gently shook food into the aquarium in my living room where I was raising Sea-Monkeys. On other mornings she had me close my eyes and imitated the feeling of raindrops falling on my back, with fluttering fingertips.

Nancy was slender and beautiful. It was kind of hard to look at her, as though I were looking at some impossibly bright light. But none of that mattered to me as much as the fact that she had the most amazing dogs I'd ever seen: a pair of borzois.

The borzoi is also known as the Russian wolfhound. The American Kennel Club describes them as "affectionate, loyal, regally dignified." What struck me about them—in addition to their obvious, eerie resemblance to Nancy herself—was that viewed from the side, they were huge, massive creatures, like balloons in a Thanksgiving parade. But as the dogs turned to face you, they virtually disappeared, so slender were they, like the dog equivalent of angelfish.

One night, we lay in my apartment in Baltimore, the borzois asleep on the floor, my fingers folded into Nancy's hair. Softly she asked, "Who *are* you, Water Strider?" The question landed heavily in the quiet room.

"I can't tell you," I said. It was the best I could do.

"You *can*," said Nancy. "You think the mist you surround yourself with is a perfect disguise. Like you're a superhero with a secret identity. But I can see you in there, James. Every now and then I catch a glimpse."

I said, "I'm no superhero, believe me."

"Come on, Water Strider, out with it. Who *are* you?"

I opened my mouth, but no words came out. How could I explain? How could I ever describe my soul with words that would not frighten this delicate person away for good?

The borzois raised their heads and looked at the two of us. We looked back at them.

There was no help for it. All I could do in the weeks to come was to quietly disappear out of Nancy's life, without an explanation. It was an unpleasant business, but it had to be done. It was a matter of national security, or so I told myself.

She was half right about me, anyhow. I did have a secret identity, but surely I was no hero.

After that, I didn't see her Russian wolfhounds anymore.

Later, I heard that she'd written a poem about me for her graduate workshop at the university, the one she was taking with David St. John. My friend Michael asked me if I wanted to read it, but I said no. I knew it would only break my heart.

She died twenty-six years later, of ovarian cancer. A friend invited me to the funeral, but I couldn't make it.

Seven years after that, while I was writing this book, in fact, it occurred to me that the poem she'd written had most likely wound up in her graduate thesis and was probably still in the Special Collections of the Johns Hopkins library. I made a single phone call to JHU, was put through to Special Collections, where a very helpful librarian—I have never met a librarian who was not helpful—said he'd find the collection for me, locate the poem, scan it, and email it to me. In less than twenty-four hours, there it was in my hands, like an artifact out of an Egyptian tomb, or a moon rock, a tiny precious thing that had been miraculously returned to me from an impossible distance.

Thirty-three years after I'd vanished on her, for committing the sin of falling in love with me, I read the words she'd written.

INCANTATION TO A MARVEL COMICS HERO

I recognized you, Water Strider,
but not right away.
I had to focus through several layers of mist
to catch the rhythm of your long legs
as you dimpled the elastic surface
between sea and air
coming toward me.

Take my hand, Water Strider,
and press the blood rising from my palm,
torn from climbing over rocks,
into the small cup you've made
of yours. Now you hold all my memories,
and we walk easily over a cold land
that was once lost to me.

Sing for me, Water Strider,
lullabies, close, so I can feel your breath
on my ear; with the notes tumbling
deep inside me, bringing the sleep

of childhood. When I wake,
feed me toast and honey
from a plate made of mermaid scales.

What shall I do for you, Water Strider?
Kiss the anger from your shoulders,
weave you a cape of ribbon grass
and fallen eyelashes
to protect you? Shall I transform my fingers
into quiet raindrops on your back?
I can do all this, Water Strider,
and still cradle the tidal pool
with your seahorse swimming in it
while you gently brush my hair.

I read these words, a description of the couple we'd been so long ago, and felt my heart clench.

I remembered Nancy Johnson, her laughter and her grace. And her dogs, both gigantic and slender.

I wanted to pick up the phone and tell her, *I'm so sorry, I should have told you. I didn't have the words then. But I have them now. Surely it's not too late, now that I've found my voice, for me to unveil the truth, for me to sing you a few of the old songs?*

But it *was* too late. This time, Nancy had ghosted me.

From Baltimore I returned to Devon frequently in 1985 and 1986, as my father got sicker and frailer. Now there were home health-care nurses attending to him. The cancer had spread to his brain. I sat by his bed as he breathed oxygen by a tube. He looked at me with his sad blue eyes, so much like my sister's. "I don't know . . . ," he said. "What is happening to me."

I held his hand.

"You'll have to take care of them," he said. "Your mother, and your sister." He squeezed my hand, hard. "Be the man."

Brown lay on the floor, jonesin' for her paws.

"The young men," my father said vaguely. "The young men shall rule."

A few days before Christmas 1985 I sat in my parents' living room, playing the piano, when a knock came on the door. I looked outside. It was a group of neighborhood carolers. They came by every year.

I swung open the door. There were all our friends, people who had watched me grow from my willowy thirteen-year-old self to whatever I was now. My mother came and stood by me, and they sang. We wrapped our arms around each other. My father lay on his deathbed one floor above us.

A sound came from upstairs—a footstep, and then another. At the top of the old stairs appeared my father, wearing his pajamas. Bald, skeletal, weightless, he descended the staircase as if he were a ghost already.

I remembered the night I had played piano in the old house *en femme* and listened as invisible footsteps came down the stairs. Was this what I had heard back then, the sound of my father's future descent? Had I been haunted back then not by some stranger from the house's past, but by the shadows of the people we were all destined to become?

We listened, the three of us, as our neighbors sang.

Myrrh is mine, its bitter perfume. Breathes a life of gathering gloom.

When they were all done, we all hugged and smiled and my father turned to my mother and me and said, "Nice tradition."

"Dick," said my mother, "you shouldn't have come down."

"Why not?" asked my father.

"Do you need help getting back to bed?"

He nodded. "You bet," he said.

Hildegarde helped him back up the stairs. I don't remember him ever coming down them again.

This, I guessed, was the kind of story the editor had in mind when she said she wanted to read something with an emotional center.

I waited until they were out of sight, then I sat down in a wing chair by the fireplace. It had been my father's chair. Grampa sneered at me from the wall. *You're not much,* he noted.

And then I started sobbing. The tears could not be quelled. Out they poured, through the fingers I held to my face, down my wrists. I shook with them, as if they might never stop. *It was sad when that great ship went down.*

A little more than a year later, I would drive north to Canada, intent on putting an end to my story. I would stand at the edge of a cliff on Cape Breton Island and stare down into the waves as a sharp breeze blew in from the North Atlantic. *Here is a song that is dumb but it's pretty. The song that the Halcyon sings by the sea.*

My father had told me that the young men would rule. But what happens when the young men aren't up to the task? What then?

It had fallen to me to look out for my mother and my sister in the years ahead. That was the mission I had accepted, when my father squeezed my hand and said, *Be the man.* But how does one learn to be a man—or, for that matter, a woman? By what process does our destiny become clear to us? What if, in spite of all our searching and wandering, our hearts refuse to reveal themselves to us? Or worse, if the demands our hearts make seem to place our very lives in danger?

I sat there under my grandfather's withering gaze. The thought of driving to Nova Scotia came to me then.

Then, unexpectedly, there was Brown. She looked at me with love and forgiveness. The dog placed her soft face in my lap.

Do not be dismayed, for I am thy Dog. Anyone who does not love does not know Dog, because Dog is love. Whoever lives in love lives in Dog, and Dog in him.

From the Penn Central tracks a mile away came the sound of a coal train passing through, on its way to Bethlehem. The engineer blew the whistle. G-major sixth.

You are not nothing, the dog suggested. *No one is nothing, if they know love.*

Brown looked at me with steadfastness and adoration, and her tail thumped against the floor. There'd been scars on her legs. But maybe, with time, they could be healed.

V

Alex, 1993

You're not lost, he said.

We were deep in it now. Alex was a Gordon setter, like a black Irish setter, a beautiful dog. I'd inherited him from my friend Zero, who'd raised him from a pup but then found, as the dog grew older and Zero's own life grew more complex, that he couldn't care for his friend anymore. And so Alex had joined me up in Maine, where I'd landed at the end of the eighties, in a farmhouse on the edge of a huge forest, married to a woman named Deirdre Finney and drunk on love and good fortune.

Now I was lost.

Alex and I worked our way through the forest. A stream trickled in the woods before us. Its waters, rich with iron, had a deep brownish-red tint. Alex turned to look at me. *You okay?*

I don't know, I told the dog. I don't know where I am.

The dog looked at me, then turned to gaze deeper into the woods. Then he froze, tail erect, one paw raised. *Look ahead.*

He held that pose for a long time. I stared in the direction of his point, but I didn't see anything. After a while Alex relaxed, turned back to me. *You didn't see it? It was right there.*

I didn't see it, I told him.

Sometimes I disappointed the dog, and this was one of those times. *You need to look harder.*

There were moments, in the late 1980s and early 1990s, when "looking harder" was not in my tool kit, and not only because I was tired of looking hard. Against all odds, a series of generous miracles had taken place in those years, and I felt as if questioning my good fortune might make it all vanish, like a magic trick that loses its charm after you learn how it is done.

Against all odds, I had found, as Evelyn Waugh had written, that *low door in the wall, which others, I knew, had found before me, which opened on an enclosed and enchanted garden, which was somewhere, not overlooked by any window, in the heart of that grey city.*

After what had felt like thirty years of wandering lost, I had fallen in love with Deedie Finney, whom in an earlier book I called "Grace." It was a good name for her. We got married. I had published a book. I got a job teaching at a college, Colby, up in Maine.

I looked around the dark forest. From somewhere in the heart of those woods I could almost hear the sound of Lloyd Goodyear drawing a bow across the strings of a cello.

Alex gave me that look again. *You're not lost,* he said.

After my father died, I did make that long trip up to Nova Scotia and stood at the edge of a cliff, looking down at the waters of the North Atlantic. On that occasion I was prevented from jumping by an invisible voice that said, *You're going to be all right. You're going to be okay.*

Whose voice was that? God's? My guardian angel's? The ghost of Dick Boylan? My future self? You can take your pick.

What I do know is that I turned around, got back in the car, and drove south for a couple of days until I showed up unexpectedly at a party in New York City, where, at a certain moment of rarefaction, I found myself alone in a dark bedroom with this girl, Deedie. I told her about the journey I'd been on.

Having lost her own mother two years before, and her father at the age of eighteen, Deedie Finney had been on a journey of her own. The summer before, she'd gotten herself halfway up Mount Rainer, ice ax in hand, before she realized she was climbing the wrong mountain. Or to be more specific, that the mountain she had to climb was not an actual mountain but something having to do with her heart.

We were married three days after my thirtieth birthday, honeymooned in Alaska, moved up to Maine, where I took on the Colby job. That same fall my first collection of short stories was published, *Remind Me to Murder You Later.*

I cannot explain how Deirdre got through to me when so many other women had not. All I can say is that I loved her more deeply than anyone I had ever known.

But I did not open my heart to her entirely, and the thing that had remained unspoken for so long stayed unsaid, even with the love of my life.

If you are wondering how anyone with such a profound and

ongoing sense of herself as trans could have failed to share this information with the woman she loves, I can only say that I had hoped then what I had hoped my whole life: that an overpowering sense of love would make me into someone else, someone better.

This might seem sad to some of you, but it also strikes me as fundamentally human. Surely the hope of being transformed by love isn't some curious delusion unique to transgender people. If you've never hoped that love would turn you into someone better, then I don't know what to tell you. We probably have different ideas about love.

Incredibly, the wish I had carried in my heart since I had sat alone inside Robotron 9000 had at last been granted, or so it then seemed. In the summer, my wife and I had long wonderful days together, and in winter, we had long wonderful nights. She made slow-cooker chili and Thai food. We drank Jameson Irish whiskey and went cross-country skiing. We ran naked through the snow and jumped into hot tubs fired by wood-burning stoves. I graded papers, and she rode horses. For Christmas she gave me a union suit—a bright red onesie with a trapdoor. As I wore this, I read the short stories of Italo Calvino while sitting in a rocking chair.

It was pretty great.

Now and again, in the middle of the night, I would open my eyes and stare at the ceiling, and the softest of voices would whisper, *You are still not you,* and in reply I would whisper back, *Shut the fuck up.* At that same moment, against the floor, I heard Alex's tail thump softly.

Did he know that I was awake? Of course he did. Alex kept one eye peeled at all times, on the off chance that, as I slept, something might come for me.

———

Back in high school, my friend Zero and I hadn't dated many girls, partly because of the depth and intimacy of our friendship with each other. All our other relationships seemed shallow compared with the baroque private world we built, a world that revolved around the music of Frank Zappa, the stories of J. R. R. Tolkien, and the delights of Panama Red. I'll always be grateful that I had a friendship as intense as the one I had with Zero when I was a teenager. But I also know that that friendship didn't leave much room for any kind of intimacy with anyone else.

One night, as I sat in Zero's high school bedroom, we listened to a band called Gong, a kind of Himalayan trance orchestra. Zero and I loved that crazy music. Sometimes our joy at hearing the music start was so great that we could not wait for the song to finish before we lifted the needle and restarted it. *I can't wait for it to be over,* Zero said to me, *so I can start it again.* We had something called a "light speaker" going in the otherwise dark room, which was a device that blinked on and off in response to the volume and texture of the music. I lay there in the flickering darkness, wishing that I could explain to my best friend the nature of what was in my heart.

The lead singer of Gong sang the words "Everything you think shows."

I sat there in the flickering darkness next to my friend and wondered if this was true.

A few years after that—during his sophomore year of college—Zero headed over to Fifield's Big M Supermarket in Syracuse, New York, to buy a carton of milk. The cashier was a red-haired punk. "Oh hey," he said to Zero. "I wanna show you this dog."

Zero asked, "What dog?"

The punk put the STATION CLOSED sign up in his lane and took Zero around to the back. Zero was still holding his milk. It was cold.

There, on the floor in front of the walk-in refrigerator, was a wild thing chained to the wall. Through a series of transparent hanging slats one could see sides of beef and boxes of frozen macaroni and cheese stacked up in the walk-in. The dog was a Gordon setter, gnawing on some gristly knuckle someone had dug out of the walk-in.

"Yeah, so I got this big stupid dog," said the punk. "His name is Alex. But he's too out of control, and my ma said I had to get him out of the house. I got him chained up back here. I was thinking maybe you all wanted to keep him?"

The Gordon setter gnawed his knuckle. He yanked and strained against his chain, howling like a creature out of Dante.

"That is one big stupid dog," said Zero.

"Tell you what," said the punk. "Whyn't you take him home for the afternoon, see what you think."

The dog bent down to lick some blood off the floor of the loading dock.

"Yeah, okay," said Zero.

How Alex went from some ogre in a walk-in refrigerator to my guardian angel, watching over his flock by night, is a complicated story, but I wasn't there in Alex's puppyhood, so I'm not the one to tell it.

I can tell you that Zero had watched over me, too, when I was a willowy teenager, and he the much cooler, much faster-talking superhero to whom I was the shy, clever sidekick. We'd seen less of each other in the years since college, but then this is so often true of the people you love the most: life takes you away.

Zero took the dog back to his hippie commune, where he lived with a half dozen lost souls and a bunch of cats and rabbits. One of the women who lived in the house—her name, incredibly, was Tonka Pooh—worked with the dog every day, showing him love, showing him consistency, until he learned how to sit and stay, to lie down and heel.

I'm not saying that any dog would have responded to this training. After all, we'd taken Brown to dog school and in the end we still had a Labrador with a lick granuloma who climbed up on top of chairs in order to turn on the kitchen spigot.

But Alex was a unique scholar, as dogs go. If you walked with him through a city, he'd immediately stop if you came to a curb, sit down, and wait until he was given the "okay" command to cross. If you told him to "stay," he'd lie himself down and stay where he'd been placed, sometimes for hours. He'd even been taught by Tonka Pooh, and others, to respond enthusiastically to a number of completely random phrases, including the words "central vacuuming" and "Popeil's Pocket Fisherman." If he heard those phrases, he'd immediately start wagging his tail joyfully, as if his entire life had been leading to one thing, and this was it.

I'd first met the dog in the early 1980s, when I'd gone to Zero's family's house in Ventnor, New Jersey. We loved going to the summer house in winter. The Atlantic City boardwalk stretched down the beachfront all the way to the border between Ventnor and Margate, and there, directly in front of the house, it came to an end. In the summer the house was abundant with grandchildren and cousins and aunts and uncles, but for most of the rest of the year, it sat there empty. Zero and I used to sneak off to the shore house during the off-season. Over the course of almost fifty years, we'd assemble there now and again to listen to the ocean, to stare into the fireplace, and to take the measure of our lives together.

We went there as teenagers, where we smoked pot and drank Mateus Rosé. The place had an amazing smell: of sea salt, and suntan lotion, and hot sand.

We went there as college students, where we read Robert Pirsig and Rabelais in front of a roaring fire.

We went there in the lost years after college, with our girlfriends: Rachel and Tonka Pooh and even a girl named Colleen, whom Zero saw for a little while. On one occasion, Colleen claimed that she'd had a visitation by the Virgin Mary. For a while it looked as though Colleen was going to have a whole transformation in the wake of this miracle. But it didn't take.

I went to that house with Deedie the New Year's after we got engaged. Years later, when I came out as trans, I gathered there with Zero and my other best friends from high school, John and Link. I sat before that same old fireplace as the boys I had known since childhood took a good long look at me, a little cupcake at last.

We went there the year we turned fifty. We went there when we turned sixty. When I am dead, I will be hurt if my friends don't gather there once more and tearfully raise a couple of jars to my insufferable genius.

For many years, there'd been one constant during our debriefs at the shore, and that was Alex. He had come there when we were all a bunch of wild-eyed hippies baking Duncan Hines yellow cakes while listening to Elton John. He had come when it was Zero and his young wife, Eve, and me and my girlfriend, Rachel; he had come when Zero was single again and it was me and my wife, Deirdre.

And on many occasions, he had been there when it was just me and Zero, two boys (*sic*) who had met each other on the first day of

summer school, June 22, 1970. It had been my twelfth birthday. There
we were, at two desks next to each other in the large study hall, in a
room with long cords dangling from the window shades, each one
hilariously tied by the schoolboys into a noose.

On Saint Stephen's Day 1978, I had sat in the living room of that
shore house as human skulls emerged from the flames in the fireplace
and circled around my head like orbiting meteors. Then they asked,
How much longer do you intend to remain content?

Alex came over, concerned. He put a tennis ball in my lap and then
gave me a look. *Remember,* he said.

I held the tennis ball in my hands, then looked at the flaming
skulls. *A little longer,* I told them. Then Alex and Zero and I had gone
outside and walked along the crashing ocean. I threw the ball. Alex
brought it back.

In some ways, what I learned about love from Alex was the same
thing I had learned from his master: that the truest measure of devotion is not complexity but constancy. It was as if we'd given each
other tenure. Even during times when we were mad at each other,
even not speaking for a few months in 1984 (Zero and Rachel didn't
get along), we always knew we would eventually find our way to each
other once more.

Alex was like that, too. If the wandering hippies started to drift too
far from the shore, he'd bring them back. If you stared too long into
the fireplace and dancing skulls emerged from the flames, Alex would
appear and drop a tennis ball into your lap.

He was good at retrieving, to be sure, and he'd bring you back a
stick or a ball or anything else that you threw. But, like his master,
Zero, a man I have loved for almost fifty years now, he was a retriever
of people, too. Because of the grace of both my friend and his dog,
I always felt that I could not be lost for long.

In 1983, Zero and I walked with Alex up on the high hill behind his house in Tully, New York. I was still working in New York and living with Rachel at the time. It was a beautiful summer day, the sun shining down all around us. Trails led through the tall grass, up to the summit.

"Listen," he said. "I think Eve and me are going to get married."

I stopped and looked at my old friend. My heart was full, but to be honest, it ached a little, too. Back then it seemed as if Zero had figured out how to do the thing that still eluded me, how to be a man in the world. Plus, I hated the fact that now there was someone that he loved more than me. It was the same sense of jealousy and loss I'd felt when my sister got married and moved away. I had a quick vision of me sitting alone at the shore house, or worse, standing by the ocean, the door of that summer house forever closed to me.

But what can you do when your best friend gets married? I tackled him and told him that I loved him. We fell into the grass together and rassled.

Alex watched us, a tennis ball in his mouth.

I didn't know Eve all that well. For a while she and Zero had been beekeepers. I have a photograph of the two of them, wearing "his" and "hers" beekeepers outfits. They made honey together, Zero and Eve. Sweet tupelo honey.

After his divorce, Zero and Alex and I gathered at the shore once more.

Zero had a friend named One Armed Bandit who was supposed to join us, too. This was a guy who'd been in a motorcycle gang, then wiped out on his Harley and lost the use of his right arm. Now it hung loosely at his side.

Of the three of us, I was the only one who was neither divorced nor a paraplegic. I had my own issues, though. Those skulls had asked, *How much longer do you intend to remain content?* and I'd put them off by saying, *A little longer.*

One Armed Bandit wasn't there when Zero and I arrived, and Zero said, Well, maybe he's not coming. At the end of day, we walked along the ocean, from Ventnor through Margate and on into Longport. Alex led the way, his tennis ball in his mouth, as I thought about my recently lost father and his commandment to *be the man.* A fierce tide was coming in as we walked, and there were some stretches along the beach where the water crashed angrily against the seawall. *You shall not pass,* said the ocean.

Alex bounded ahead through the foam, turned back, and looked at us. *You're going to make it,* he suggested somberly.

We walked past Lucy the Elephant, the six-story elephant hotel from the nineteenth century that is now a tourist attraction and curiosity. Between our freshman and sophomore years, Zero and I had worked at Lenny's Hot Dog stand directly next to Lucy. We worked the midnight to 5:00 A.M. shift, making hot dogs, roasting hot pretzels. The big rush came at 4:00 A.M. when the disco across the street closed and all the coked-out disco dancers came up to Lenny's window. I had worked the corn window. Zero worked the grill in the room the Lenny's workers called the "hemina-hemina room," because the intensity of everyone yelling while the hot dogs sizzled and the onion rings boiled in the hot fat fryer invoked the memory of a very nervous Ralph Kramden saying just this: *Hemina-hemina-hemina.*

Alex led us past Lucy, past the shuttered shell of Lenny's, past the beachfront homes of Longport, until at last we came to a pier at the end of the island, where Alex sat down and dropped his ball between his paws, and Zero and I sat down and watched the sun set over the ocean. The sky turned crimson, then purple, then gray. We put our arms around each other's backs. A cold wind blew.

Then Zero picked up the ball and threw it into the sea. Alex leapt in, disappeared beneath the waves for a moment, then climbed out of the ocean with the ball in his mouth. He came back to us, dropped the ball at our feet. Then he shook. Salt water flew in every direction.

Alex took a step back. His tail grew erect. He raised his front paw. The Gordon setter pointed at the ball. *Look,* he suggested, his whole attention fixated upon it. *It's here.*

Later, we headed home again: past Lenny's, past Lucy the Elephant, past the high stone wall where once again the voice of the sea said, *You shall not pass.* Alex had the tennis ball in his mouth. The ocean roared.

Zero had been in love, and then his marriage had ended. My father had died, and I felt the impossible burden of things I knew I needed to do but could not do. The sun set over the ocean behind us, and our shadows grew long. We walked toward them.

Alex kept close watch on us as we made our way along the shore once more. Concerned lest we should stumble.

When the house was almost in sight, Zero stopped in his tracks and looked up at the skies in wonder. "The stars," he said. "Look at all the stars." He pointed at the heavens and showed me Orion, sinking now in the late spring sky, and the rising constellations of summer: the Lion and Perseus. For a while we stood there, two old friends, stunned at the universe.

When we finally arrived home, the One Armed Bandit was sitting on the front porch. His dead arm dangled by his side.

"Gentlemen," he said.

He'd been a young dog in the late 1970s and had seen us through the adventures and mistakes of the next dozen-odd years. But by 1992, Alex lay surrounded in a cloud of his own flatulence on the floor of the little house in which Deedie and I lived in Maine. He had long black feathering on the backs of his legs and on his ears, although some of it was now gray. His brown eyes shone.

"Whoa," said Deedie, waving her hand through the air. "He's especially—fragrant tonight."

"He is," I said. "You think that's lucky?"

Deedie smiled, opening the package she'd purchased at the Rite Aid earlier that day. "Hope so," she said, and headed off to the bathroom.

Another wave of stench wafted from the dog. In his dotage, Alex had developed a signature odor, the result of a skin condition that could apparently not be cured. Every week or so we gave the old dog a special bath, lathering him up with a special shampoo, but if this had any beneficial effects, they were outrun within a couple of days. For a long time I'd taken Alex with me to the English Department at Colby, where I'd become that adorable professor who takes his dog to work. Alex was good as gold for the longest time, staying where he'd been told to stay for hours at a time, as I went off to teach classes or attend meetings. But one day, one of my colleagues—Cedric Bryant, a seven-foot-tall African American Americanist—came by my office to have a serious talk with me. "Listen, Jim," he said. "That dog is *ripe*."

We knew that Alex wouldn't be around much longer, and not only because he smelled like rotting ham. After all these years, he was finally slowing down. Plus, it's not unlikely that his heart was broken after being sent to our house in Maine to retire. We loved Alex and did everything we could for him. But we knew we were not his first loves and that even now he hoped, in his quiet, stoic manner, that Zero one day might yet come back for him.

I was thirty-five years old. Deedie and I had been married for five years. The days of sneaking off to Zero's shore house to drink Mateus Rosé were almost half my lifetime away.

I bent down and rubbed Alex's belly. "I'm sorry you smell," I said.

Deedie came back, holding the pregnancy test in one hand. She showed it to me. It was negative. For now.

"Okay," said the vet a few weeks later. "Let's get him up on the table."

We were in a small chamber, Deirdre and Alex and the vet and me, and a stainless-steel platform was affixed to one of the cinder-block walls. It was a sad place.

"I can't lift him by myself."

"You get his front, I'll get his back," said the vet. Alex was a big dog. We squatted down and gave him the heave-ho. He didn't struggle. He lay down on the metal table and looked us in the eyes. *You're going to be all right,* the dog suggested. *There will be others.*

"I'm just going to shave a small area on his leg," said the vet, turning on a pair of surgical snippers.

My wife and I looked at each other, as if hoping that somehow, even now, there might be an alternative to the fate that lay directly ahead. Zero had felt this same impulse a week or two earlier, when we'd called him on the phone to let him know what was about to transpire. "Yeah," he said. "Well, what if I could . . . nurse him back to health?"

He hadn't seen Alex for a while now and didn't know how far his old friend had fallen. So perhaps he could be forgiven for not understanding that the days when Alex might have been nursed back to health were long gone. It's a human impulse, I reckon. Years and years later, as I sat by the side of my dying mother, I thought something along the same lines. It wasn't as if, at age ninety-four, Hildegarde was leaving us too soon. And yet, instead of preparing myself for the inevitable, I found my thoughts running toward the miraculous. What if my mother gave up gluten? Was it so impossible that that might restore her, even now that her internal organs were shutting down and she had lost the ability to speak?

Still, I suppose the belief in the impossible is a sign of human resilience, rather than idiocy. If it is possible that the universe itself is the result of a primordial singularity, a moment at which all known things began to expand from a single point of energy and light and heat—then who is to say that a dying dog might not yet be healed by love? Is the transformative power of love so much more unlikely than the Big Bang? You tell me.

I wasn't around during the Big Bang—at least not in this form, anyhow—so I can't say. But I have seen love make some things come into being that you seriously would not believe.

"Okay," said the vet. "Are you ready for me to give him the injection now?"

"Jim," said Deedie, and we clutched on to each other like survivors of a shipwreck desperately grasping the same floating two-by-four in the midst of a vast and terrible sea. Alex was still giving me that look. *It's all right*, he said. *You will know many dogs.*

It's been said that one reason we don't remember the pain of childbirth is that if we did, no one would ever go through it more than once. Losing a dog is like that, too. I'm pretty sure that if I remembered the terrible details of those losses more clearly, I would never have taken in another puppy. You wonder, as you stand there with your friend up on the table, if all those good years justify this one horrific moment.

The vet looked at me. "Are we ready?" he asked again.

I felt like General Longstreet when Pickett asked him if he should make his charge. I'd lost the ability to speak. So, like Longstreet, I just nodded.

I couldn't wait for it to be over, so I could start it again.

Zero hadn't been back to Syracuse for a long time. He had a few friends still in the area—most of them chefs and nightclub owners. So we drove back there one golden autumn day, my old friend and I, and once again walked up through the hills of Tully.

In one hand I carried an Autoharp in a little suitcase. In the other I had Alex's ashes in a large cookie tin. They were heavier than I'd expected.

We'd parked our car on the far side of the mountain, opposite from the place where he used to live, and began to hike up the old familiar paths. Somewhere along here was the place where, when I'd learned he was getting married, back in the early 1980s, I'd tackled him and we'd rolled around together in the tall brown weeds.

A little way up the path we were suddenly accosted by a small Boston terrier. He looked at us and said, "Yap."

"Hey, look," said Zero. "It's Scrap."

"Scrap?" I said. "Do you know this dog?"

"Loosely speaking," he said.

We walked up the path, Scrap trailing us, growling softly. It was a little unnerving. "No," I said. "What I mean is, is this a dog you've met before?"

"Not while I was awake," said Zero.

"So what's the deal?" Scrap was still on our heels. We climbed farther up the mountain, Alex's ashes in my hands.

"I think he's our spirit guide."

I looked back at the irritated, territorial Scrap. "Yeah, well, if he is our spirit guide, I wouldn't be a bit surprised."

"Yap," said Scrap.

The three of us climbed up the hill, breathing heavily, until at last Zero raised one hand. "Sshhh," he said. We crept forward. Scrap growled quietly. My friend parted the long grass with his hands. In the valley below us was the house where he'd lived a long time ago, back when he first got married. Somewhere down there were the ruins of some old beehives.

"I wonder who lives there now," Zero said. "Some strangers, maybe?"

Scrap grabbed the cuff of my pants and tugged on it. "Rrrrr," said Scrap.

We pulled back and let the weeds obscure the house where Zero had once lived. We walked back up the path a little bit, and there before us was the big flat rock. I remembered this from a long time ago.

"Okay," said Zero, and he took the cookie tin from me and opened it up and dumped the ashes on the rock. They were very white. There wasn't much dog in them.

"We used to play a lot of stick up here," said my friend, and his voice caught. "Him and me." We sat down on the rock and watched the wind blow the ashes.

Then I got out the Autoharp. Once it had belonged to Link, but I'd "borrowed" it over Christmas break during my senior year at Wesleyan, and it had never made it back to him. I put picks on my fingers and my thumb, and I started to play.

> *From this valley they say you are leaving.*
> *We will miss your bright eyes and sweet smile.*
> *For they say you are taking the sunshine*
> *That has brightened our pathways a while.*

Scrap listened to all of this with a fairly tolerant expression, given his apparent contempt for us.

"Come on," said Zero, and I put the Autoharp back in the suitcase and we walked back down the mountain, Scrap nipping at our heels. Zero held the cookie tin, now empty, in one hand.

"Yap," said Scrap.

"You know," I said to Zero, "maybe Scrap here needs a home."

"What?" he said with an air of incredulity.

"Yap," noted Scrap.

"Maybe there's a reason he's appeared to us, and come along with us on this journey. Maybe all he needs is a little love."

Zero stopped in his tracks, looked at me hard, looked down at Scrap. I wondered whether he was remembering many years before, when he had been led by a young red-haired punk out to the loading dock of Fifield's Big M and found a big stupid dog licking blood off the floor of a walk-in refrigerator.

"You," said my friend, "are out of your mind."

We carried on our way, Zero out front, me in the rear, Scrap between us. It occurred to me, as we descended from the place of Alex's last end, that if Zero *did* adopt this Scrap, it wouldn't be more than a couple of years before ownership of Scrap would pass to me. How long would it be before Scrap had to be "sent to a farm"? How much time would pass before the beings that had to be sent to a farm were Zero and myself?

If you think about it that way, I guess everybody's got a farm waiting.

We came down off the mountain. There was our car, parked at the end of the fire road. Zero opened the door to his vehicle, and we looked around for our spirit guide.

But Scrap had disappeared.

"Well," said Zero, "I guess he felt his work was done."

We didn't say anything as we drove back into town. Zero went down Greenmont Street, took a left into the parking lot of Fifield's Big M. Across the street was the hippie house he'd lived in so long ago and the big park behind that. We got out of the car, walked around the back to the loading dock. After all this time, we were back where we had started.

There was a small Dumpster out back. Zero took the Christmas cookie tin, opened the Dumpster, and gently slipped it in. Then we got back in the car.

"Well," he said as we turned out onto the road, "I guess that's that."

We left that mountain and went out to dinner in Syracuse at a restaurant owned by a man named Patrick. He was the brother of Colleen, the woman who'd seen the Virgin Mary. I didn't know Patrick all that well. I knew that he'd been sick with cancer and that now, for a little while anyhow, he was better.

Once, though, he'd been on hand during one of those trips to the seashore, back in the 1980s when we were all so young and lost and full of beans. There had been, perhaps, a dozen of us that year—me and Zero, Steve Mo the chef and his wife, Liza, a couple named Sharon and Popeye, and of course One Armed Bandit, and some other folks I did not know called the Cake People.

And Alex. He lay, mostly, on a circular dog bed by the fireplace, looking up now and again to make sure everyone was staying in line. We cooked a big lasagna, drank some red wine. The Cake People made cake. We told a few stories, and a few songs were sung—I remember singing "The Wren," an old folk song about Twelfth Night. *Joy, health, love, and peace be all here in this place.*

It has been a long time since that New Year's—at least thirty, maybe thirty-five years, and the young twentysomethings whom I put my arms around that night are mostly in their sixties now—the ones who lived, that is.

Snow began to fall and we looked out the windows at the flakes gathering on the sand. At midnight we put on our coats and mittens and stumbled out onto the beach, where the snow by now was almost ankle deep. The waves crashed right up into the snow, making that eternal note of sadness Matthew Arnold was so fond of. We were a shaggy, rangy group of young people, dancing to music that only we could hear, embracing each other, leaping, shouting, falling down in the sandy snow, and lying there watching the flakes come down and melt upon our skin. At last we all gathered together and sang "Will the Circle Be Unbroken?" *There's a better home a-waiting, in the sky, Lord, in the sky.*

Our arms were around each other's backs. Our breath came out in clouds. "Alex," Zero called. "Alex?"

The circle broke as we looked for the dog.

He was standing by the ocean in full point position, tail erect, one paw raised. As if whatever it was we were all searching for could be found there, beyond the cruel Atlantic, beyond the unreachable horizon.

Zero finally found the love of his life in his late forties, a woman who, eerily, had the same name as me. I was happy for both of them. Zero and Jen were married on a beautiful day in Cape Ann, in Massachusetts, on a bank overlooking the sea.

From where we stood, we could see some rocks offshore where, according to legend, the *Hesperus* had been wrecked during the Blizzard of 1839. All hands aboard had been lost. A woman had washed ashore, still tied to the mast.

I'd been his best man back in 1983. Back then, I'd been too self-conscious and sad to make a toast.

This time, I got to sign the *ketubah*.

A couple of years later, Zero went to a Buddhist retreat in South America for a few days. In one of the sessions, the monk had asked him to visualize in his mind a person whom he believed to be a saint.

Later, when he told me this story, I had been hurt by it, a little bit, and I told my friend as much.

"Why are you hurt?" he asked, baffled.

"Well, you said that when you visualized the person you imagined to be a saint, you said—what was it? A face appeared out of the darkness? A big pink tongue? Long black ears, a mouth holding a tennis ball?"

"Yeah, Jenny," he said wearily. "That's what I saw. Why would that hurt you?"

"I don't know," I said self-consciously. "I guess because when you told me about imagining someone whom you believed to be a saint, for a second I thought maybe you were thinking—of me?"

Zero laughed.

"You?" he said. "Yeah, right."

VI

Lucy, 1999

You know, your problem, said Russo,
is that you think it is realism.

The hair on Lucy's back rose up like a Mohawk and she raised her head from the blue rug where she lay. From out in the driveway came the idling of a truck.

A man in brown stood on the porch. "United Parcel," said he, and handed me the package. Lucy, a medium-sized yellow dog with a purple tongue, barked at him with heartbroken rage.

"Hush," I said to the dog as the truck drove off. "It's okay."

In my hands I held the cardboard box. It had come from far away.

Inside the box were all the things you'd need if you wanted to be somebody else.

Lucy growled. I stood there with the box in my hands, my heart pounding.

It's okay? the dog said. She knew full well what the box held: a wig, a pair of false eyelashes, a pair of large-sized shoes. *In what possible world is it okay?*

I had found the ad in the Kennebec *Morning Sentinel,* back in 1991. *Golden Retriever pups,* it said. *AKC certified. Weaned and wormed. $50. Call Ruben Flood at the Bacon Farm.*

I loved the *Morning Sentinel,* read it cover to cover every morning. My favorite column was the "Police Log," which was a daily summary of criminal activity in Kennebec County, Maine. One such entry read, *Officers summoned to Davis Launderette. Man found wearing only plastic garbage bag. Officers issued a warning. And suggested next time man not wash the clothes he was wearing.*

I got a pen and circled the classified ad for the golden retriever puppies.

Deedie was away that summer, in grad school at the Smith College School for Social Work. We'd moved into our new house in Belgrade Lakes that May, and even though we had barely unpacked our boxes, soon it was time for her to head off for the summer session at Smith. It seemed cruel that the two of us, having found each other after no small measure of loss in both of our lives, would find ourselves torn apart again so soon.

And so off she had headed for the green pastures of Northampton, leaving me alone in our new house—alone, that is, except for the flatulent Alex, who by now spent most of his days lying on his side, dreaming softly of Zero and the green fields of Syracuse. I watched her drive away, the both of us crying, and then I went back inside. I went up to the second floor and opened the window. Then I climbed out onto the roof and followed it up to the ridge and sat there with my back against the chimney.

It was so quiet in Maine. Our house had a big green lawn, maybe three acres in all, and the house was set well back from the road. A stream rushed just beyond the tree line to the right. And on all sides were the thick trees, untamed forest in which dwelled coyotes and eagles and moose.

The moose would occasionally lumber into our backyard—always a cow, never a bull—and they would stand there chewing moss. We didn't see them that often, but we knew they were there. We'd hear the sound as they crashed through the thick, tangled forest.

I sat there in the June sunshine with my back against the chimney. Not far from where I sat was a weather vane we'd purchased at a lawn sale, a copper moose upon an arrow that twisted with the wind. My heart had pounded in my chest as I'd screwed it into the ridge a few weeks before. I could see the driveway below me as I worked, and I suddenly understood how precarious my position was, how just a few inches separated me from a long drop down to the earth.

I was greeted at the Bacon Farm by Ruben Flood, an enormous man wearing a pair of worn denim overalls and no shirt. His chest hair curled upon the generous mounds of his pectorals like pieces of shaved coconut upon an elaborate human cake.

Mr. Flood led me past the sties and barns filled with oinking and squealing. At the time I had forgotten exactly how large hogs could grow, if you gave them half a chance. But once reacquainted with this fact, I have never forgotten it. According to my records here, there was once a pig named Reggie at the Iowa State Fair in 2012 that tipped the scales at 1,335 pounds. Although that was still in the future, in the new century that even in the 1990s still seemed unimaginable, like something out of a science-fiction movie.

There's nothing subtle about a pigsty, and the smell of the marshy, fetid quagmire where the hogs of Ruben Flood resided was enough to set a person back some. Ruben didn't seem affected by it, though. He just kept waddling past the sties until we arrived at a stone building not so unlike the milk house up in Earle's Woods, where once Lloyd Goodyear and Playboy and I had stumbled upon the lesbians and their Harley. Inside was a small pen, and in the pen, all alone, was a small yellow puppy. She was standing when we entered the outbuilding, but when she saw us, she sat down and raised her head hopefully.

"She's the lahst one," said Mr. Flood, who featured the kind of deep, Down East accent that is actually something of a rarity outside of Pepperidge Farm commercials. "Othas went upta the naybuhs."

I leaned down. The puppy was a small yellow fluff ball. She stood up on her hind legs, resting her front paws on the chicken wire of her enclosure. I looked at Mr. Flood. "Can I hold her?" I said.

"Ayuh," he said, and I thought, *"Ayuh," seriously?*

Mr. Flood reached down into the pen, which was no small feat given his size. I was expecting him to hand the dog to me, but instead he just held her to his chest, stroking her soft ruff. The puppy whimpered softly. Then, suddenly, the light in the place dimmed.

"Ruben!" said a voice, and we turned to see a figure standing in the doorway. This, I presumed, was Mrs. Flood, and she was, incredibly, even larger than her husband. She, too, was wearing a pair of stained overalls, and in one hand she held a large metal rake, which I could only assume, from the pig shit attached to its impressive iron tines, was a device for moving hog effluvium from one place to another. "What are you doing in here!" she said.

"I'm—looking at this puppy?" I said, uncertain whether this was clear or not. But Mrs. Flood wasn't talking to me.

"Evah time I look up, you're in heeyah with these *creachas!*" she said. Her anger seemed out of proportion to the situation, which led me to guess that it wasn't the situation with the golden retriever pups that had gotten her goat; it was, instead, a long trail of grievances involving her wedded husband in which I was only the most recent complication.

"Just sellin' the lahst'un," said Mr. Flood, looking down at the puppy.

"I can come back," I said, embarrassed that I'd somehow stumbled into what kind of felt like an Edward Albee play set on a hog farm.

"You make sure the deal he give you is *fayah!*" said Mrs. Flood, and then struck the cement floor with the handle of her rake. A little of the pig shit impaled upon the tines fell off of it. Then she turned around and went back outside, and the place filled with light again.

"Your ad said fifty dollars?" I said.

"Ayuh," said Mr. Flood. "She's got 'er shots. Wormed up, too," he said. "She's the lahst one. Othas went upta naybahs." He was still holding the puppy on his chest, cradling her over his heart.

"Well, I'll take her, if it's really okay."

"She's a good pup," he said, and unless I was mistaken, his eyes were shimmering. "Had fowah that lived in the littah," he said. "She's the lahst."

I handed him $50, and for a moment he seemed reluctant to take the money. But then he stuffed it into the pocket of his overalls with one hand, while still cradling the pup to his chest with the other. "Okay," he said. He looked the little dog in her face. "You be a good dog now. Remembah what I told yah."

He handed me the puppy, and now it was my turn to hold her to my chest. "What did you tell her?" I asked as we walked back outside into the putrid-smelling atmosphere of the hog farm.

Mr. Flood made a sound that I realized was laughter. "That's between me and huh," he said.

As I walked to my car I saw Mrs. Flood standing in a pigsty, surrounded by enormous hogs. She was raking the ground. She glanced up at me threateningly as I passed. Behind her was their trailer. The door was open. Several cats skulked in and out.

As I got to the car I turned back to find Mr. Flood looking longingly at me and the puppy. It was as if his heart were breaking, as if I were removing the last thing from his life that was not a hog or his wife. "Hey," I said. "Would it be okay if I took your picture?" I had my camera in the car.

"Uh," said Mr. Flood. "I don't think so. I don't like having my *pitcha* taken much."

I thought about this, then nodded. "Okay," I said. "Thanks." I got in the car and put the puppy in a small cardboard box I'd left on the passenger seat. I got the Volkswagen turned around and headed back out to the main road. The last thing I saw, in the rearview mirror, was Mr. Flood standing by the barn, watching me drive off with the dog. Mrs. Flood was standing behind *him*, raking the rank, damp earth.

That night, I sat in my living room with the puppy, whom I decided to name Ruby. I'd purchased a small crate, which I imagined the dog would welcome as a soothing, den-like home, as well as a goodly portion of bagged-up puppy chow. Ruby had walked around sniffing everything and whimpering softly. "It's okay," I told the dog. "I just moved here, too."

Alex, deep into his dotage by now, was far from certain about having a puppy in his life. I suppose it was sort of like meeting the person they've hired to replace you just before you retire. Or, like Gene Kelly in *Singin' in the Rain,* facing the fresh-faced version of his former nerdlike self: *"Gotta dance!"* He sat down in the middle of the kitchen with his tennis ball in his mouth, making it clear to the puppy that in spite of his generous character there were some things he would not be sharing and that his tennis ball was one of them.

I called Deedie on the phone and reached her in her dormitory at Smith College, a building called Martha Washington that, in the summers, was filled with hundreds of social-workers-to-be. "You'll never guess what I did today," I said to my bride. I was so excited to tell her about the Floods and their hog farm.

"What?" said Deedie.

"I got a puppy!" I blurted out. "A little golden retriever! Her name is Ruby!"

There was silence on the line. It wasn't what I was expecting.

"Hello?" I said.

Several days later, I locked Ruby up in the crate, then rode my bicycle to a bar. It was one of the delights of our new house, that the Sunset Grill was just a mile away and that when the mood took me, I could head down to the bar and have a pint in about as long as it took to open a can of dog food.

It would be at this very same bar, ten years later, that I would sit on a stool reviewing the instructions from my doctor.

Let us pause at this moment to consider the future that awaited me.

There I am in 2001, sitting on my stool, holding a rather graphic sketch of the area that in Ireland is referred to as "down below" and that addresses details of a particular dilemma presented by the forthcoming surgery. The specific complication in this instance was that *after all was said and done,* some of what was currently on the outside of this area would take up new residence on the inside, and in order to ensure that one's interior regions were—in the words of my surgeon—"pink and mucosal," it would be necessary to make sure that they were hairless before the doctor embarked upon the dipsy-doodle. The instructions in my hand at the bar included a hand-drawn sketch that it was impossible to gaze upon without equal measures of horror and wonder.

I would take these instructions to heart, although finding an electrologist who was willing to work in such an intimate way was far from easy, especially in a place as remote as northern New England. My regular electrologist, in Waterville, had been helpful enough when it was my face that was being smoothed, but when I raised the prospect of *down below* she just shook her head. "I don't *think* so," said she.

As with so many aspects of this process back then, I finally got wind of a woman up for the challenge through some of the other trans women I knew, through a series of whispers and secret signals reminiscent of the French underground or the ancient order of Freemasons. This woman worked out of a trailer in a town called Livermore Falls, a hard-bitten mill town where my band had once played in a bar called Ma Duck's. There really was a Ma Duck, too, a tough woman who walked around with a baseball bat making sure that nobody got any ideas. The electrologist's trailer was just a few miles out of town. It was to her practice I would make my way that dark, cold winter and present myself for electrocution. In preparation for this, I had been prescribed something called Emla cream, which essentially numbed the skin that was being smelted. Then, in order to keep it all from rubbing off upon my underpants during the hour-long drive between our house in Belgrade Lakes and the secret trailer in Livermore Falls, I had to first apply the cream to the area in question and then enclose this selfsame organ with Saran wrap. I am sorry to say that during this season we had purchased plastic that was tinted with something called "ruby laser red." And so thus bemummified, I drove to Livermore Falls, Maine, in the subzero Maine winter, the wind howling outside. I pulled up at the trailer and walked inside. There I took off my clothes and I laid myself down for sacrifice.

The woman who was working upon me liked to listen to English handbell music. She had dozens of CDs, which we listened to in rotation as she proceeded with the task before her. This always began with her unwrapping the ruby laser red wrap from the unit in question, as if it were Christmas morning and she the luckiest princess in all of Livermore Falls.

There I lay, four hours per session, listening to English handbell ringers perform the music of Vivaldi, Corelli, and Telemann, my nether parts shiny with anesthetizing nougat, my electrologist attending to me with a burning hot needle, as outside crystal snowflakes the size of Roosevelt dimes shattered against her trailer's plate-glass windows. On her boom box played *Miserere mei, Deus*. With every single molten electrification of the needle, I would recoil in agony, as though I'd just been jolted with a pair of defibrillator paddles.

This went on for four hours. That Emla cream took some of the sting out of things. But not enough.

Tears rolled out of my eyes and bled down the sides of my face. By the time the session was over, my head was sitting in a small pool of salt water. I lay there sobbing, but the pain I was feeling was really not the worst of it. What I also considered, with each convulsing electrical blast, was that this long journey itself might result in the loss of everything and everyone I had ever loved.

Years and years later, my friend Kate Bornstein told me she was working on a book called *Trans! Just for the Fun of It!*

I am glad it was fun for somebody.

"Pope Urban loved this piece so much," said my electrologist, "that for years he wouldn't let it be played anywhere except the Sistine Chapel."

Ice crystals dinged against the window. "You sure know a lot about—" She zapped me again, and I recoiled with the pain. "Baroque music," I said.

"Mostly what I like is English handbells," she said. "It's like the music—"

Once more she jolted me with electricity.

"—of the angels."

But all of this was in the future. Let us return to 1991, when I was still just another guy at a bar. I had a plaid shirt, a mop of brown hair.

I put down my pint and paid my bill. And then I was back on my bicycle, ascending the hill that led from the Sunset Grill and back to our house on Castle Island. It took longer to get back home than it had to leave, what with the wobbles.

I opened the door to find Alex on the floor with a look of exhaustion and resignation upon his old-dog face. The puppy was howling piteously.

"Lucy!" I shouted. "I'm home!"

Alex looked at me uncertainly. *I thought you said her name was Ruby.*

So I did, I thought. I opened the crate. The dog-training book I'd been consulting had insisted that puppies wouldn't crap up their crate, because it was intrinsic to them that the den was a place they kept pristine.

But the authors of my dog book—a group of dog mystics named the Monks of New Skete—had never had a puppy like Ruby, or Lucy, as it was now clear to me she should be named instead. I reached into the crate and pulled out the puppy, covered from tail to muzzle in her own *ejectamenta*. I thought of Mrs. Flood, standing there with her metal rake. Was this what happened when a dog's formative days were spent upon a hog farm? Was this what happened when your only friends were seven-hundred-pound pigs?

I washed the puppy off in the sink. Then I took her outside and let her run around on our big green lawn. I sat there on the porch and watched the little dog. She bit a dandelion, then paused to look back at me. It was as if she were considering me for the first time.

What is it, girl? I said. Tell me.

The dog seemed to reach a conclusion. *I hate you,* she said.

"She's a pretty good dog," said John P the Dog Man. "She's got real potential."

From the way he said it, it didn't seem like a compliment. But then the Dog Man set the bar high. He had about fifty dogs of his own, most of them a breed called Plott hound, which I'd never heard of. They were big lunky things.

All summer long I'd applied the method the Monks of New Skete had recommended with Lucy, but as she grew it became clearer and clearer that she had very little interest in the monastic lifestyle.

"She doesn't have respect for you," said the Dog Man, after analyzing my interaction with Lucy. "She needs to know that when you're talking, you're giving her Words of Command."

"But why?" I said, surely echoing the words of my own parents after they returned from New Orleans to discover that my sister and

I had had a party in their absence, during which Moey had put a rock through the windshield of Lisa Boyer's Volkswagen. "What have I done to earn her disrespect?"

"I don't know," said the Dog Man. "But you're sending her a message, somehow."

"What message am I sending her?" I said, feeling somehow on the defensive here.

John P the Dog Man was a strange mixture of childlike glee and mysticism. You could tell he loved spending his entire day working with dogs. But the connection he had with them—and not just his own but all dogs—seemed to verge upon the metaphysical. Lucy, at the other end of a leash held by John P the Dog Man, turned into a completely different creature. She stayed. She heeled. She sat. She'd have read *The New Yorker* if he'd handed her a copy. Even when she was lying down, her eyes followed John P the Dog Man everywhere he went, as if she'd been hypnotized. Every order he gave her, Lucy responded with the dog equivalent of *Yes, master.*

"I don't know," said John P the Dog Man. "Somehow she thinks you're telling her that you don't deserve respect."

"Wait," I said. "John. Are you telling me that Lucy believes—that I don't respect myself?"

John P smiled his puppy dog smile. "I don't know," he said. "Do ya?"

Large Mr. Flood had not told the whole truth in his classified ad in the *Morning Sentinel,* as became self-evident as the puppy grew larger and with each passing day resembled something that was not exactly a golden retriever. For one thing, her coat was more yellow than golden, and her hair was short, like a Lab's, rather than the thick mane of a golden. And she never quite attained the full height of a retriever, either; she got to be about three-quarters that size and then quit, perhaps taking inventory of the world around her and concluding, *What's the point?*

Plus, her tongue was purple.

When friends would notice this odd detail, they would not infrequently declare, "She's half chow chow!" For some reason, this always irritated me. It was bad enough that I'd gone out to buy a golden retriever and come home with something that was not; but that I'd been unable, apparently, to perceive the difference between a golden retriever and something that was half chow chow was a humiliation I found it hard to shoulder.

She also had none of the eagerness to please that I associate with goldens. Instead, she was a hardheaded, opinionated individual that considered all of our suggestions for her behavior to be distantly amusing, like the antics of a fop in a 1930s screwball comedy. Hour after hour I'd walk her through the paces taught to us by John P the Dog Man, and at the end of our tutorial, when I'd unclip Lucy from her leash, she'd just wander off into the woods, while I shouted at her, "No! Come back! Lucy, come!"

The dog would pause at the edge of our property to look back at me, to let me know she'd heard my Words of Command. Then she'd give me a look that said, *As if*, and disappear into the woods. Sometimes she'd come back after an hour or so. Other times it would be longer.

Deedie returned from her summer at Smith and in no time at all opened her heart to Lucy, in spite of the fact that I had adopted the dog without her consultation. Soon enough, in fact, she seemed to have a slightly better relationship with Lucy than I did.

They may have bonded because Deedie took a long walk with Lucy each morning, as the sun rose through the pines. But it might also be because of the words that John P the Dog Man had spoken. In Deedie the dog saw someone who respected herself, a woman who Knew Who She Was.

Which is more than we could say about some people.

The dog had one unique talent, which was the uncanny ability to catch flies with her mouth, as if she were a dragonfly or some breed of exotic long-tongued frog. To Lucy they were not flies; they were *Sky Raisins.*

When strangers asked us what kind of dog Lucy was, we'd say, *She's a Kennebec Valley Flycatcher.* Sometimes people would respond by saying, *Really? I've never heard of that breed of dog.*

To which we could only reply, *Yeah, well. We hadn't heard about it either.*

I took Lucy down to my mother's house in Pennsylvania one summer trip. There, around a dinner table, my mother told the story of how I'd bought the dog from a pig farmer, some character who'd charged me $500 for what was supposed to be a golden retriever but was actually a *chow chow.* She laughed heartily, as my mother liked to do, at the idea of my obliviousness.

Later, I told my mother it was $50, not $500.

My mother held my shoulder and smiled. "I know, honey," she said. "But it's a better story this way. That's the important thing, the story!"

Maybe you wonder how I wound up this way? This is how.

Each of my dogs had provided me with a kind of moral instruction—from the consequences of unrequited love (Sausage) to the delights of unrestrained desire (Matt); from the virtue of loyalty (Alex) to the tragedy of obsession (Brown). Lucy was the first dog that was mine, whom I had chosen as an adult, and I'd imagined that I'd be able to take everything I'd learned from all the dogs that had come before her and use this knowledge to create a better kind of relationship.

But it wasn't long before I realized that, once again, my dog had a very different idea of what that relationship might be. Lucy, as it turned out, would measure everything by the hog-farm standard— and no matter what I did, no matter how many hours I spent working with her, training her, giving her all my love, it was clear in the end that our little house on Castle Island Road was never going to be as satisfying as the Bacon Farm.

Was it that Ruben Flood and his enormous wife had set the bar incredibly high—perhaps feeding their not-exactly-golden-retriever pups the same exotic slops they'd given to their hogs? Maybe there was something about the smell of the sty, the warmth of straw, the gurgling of warm mud, that filled Lucy's heart in a way that could never be filled by us.

But I suspect that it's not that the love of Ruben Flood was so much better than the love Lucy received from Deedie and me. More likely it's just that a hog farm was what she loved first, and there's something about first loves that we carry the rest of our days.

Maybe that's what Ruben Flood whispered in Lucy's ear that day I picked her up at the farm. *You can nevah love anotha.*

Even now, at age sixty, I can find myself waking from a dream about Shannon, that girl I crushed out on so deeply in high school. It's sad, really. We look all around us, at the miracles made possible by the lives we have created. We fight so hard to achieve the success we dreamed of. And even surrounded by the world that this love has made possible, sometimes we look wistfully through the rain-streaked window and think, *I still wish I had what I had when I was young.*

Oh, if only tomorrow I could wake up in warm straw, surrounded by pigs.

"Down," said Deedie, issuing a Word of Command. Lucy bounced up and down at the other end of the leash. We were standing on the threshold of the house of her childhood friend Chelsea, in Cleveland Heights, Washington, D.C. As Lucy hit the ground, some menstrual dog blood dripped out her back end and fell in an astonishing red drop on the flagstone.

"Uh-oh," I said. We'd just rung the doorbell, and from inside we heard the sound of approaching footsteps.

"You don't know Chelsea," said Deedie, which was only half true. She'd been one of the maids of honor when we got married, and I'd spent an evening or two during our courtship with her. Chelsea and her family were some of Deedie's oldest friends. After Deedie had been orphaned at a relatively young age, Chelsea's parents—along with a few other devoted Washington friends of the Finney family—had tried to step into the gap left by Tom and Sally Finney's absence.

The door swung open. There was Chelsea's mother, Shirley, who even at this midday hour looked elegant. Chelsea was coming down the stairs behind her, looking just as poised. Even before I entered the house I could see that everything in it was carefully arranged. It was like something out of *Architectural Digest.*

"Deirdre!" said Shirley.

"Deedie!" shouted Chelsea.

Everyone hugged my wife. I stood behind her with the dog on a leash, bouncing up and down. Another drop of Lucy fell upon the flagstones. "Hello, James!" said Shirley, and I leaned in for a hug. "Come in! Come in!"

I looked at the floor. It was a pure white carpet, thick and rich. I looked at the dog. Then I looked at the carpet again.

"And who do we have here?" asked Shirley, bending down to pat the dog on the head.

"This is Lucy," I said.

"She's divine!" said Chelsea.

"Come in!" said Shirley.

"Okay," I said, and in we went.

In the living room was a Christmas tree out of *Martha Stewart Living,* glowing with illuminated lamps in the shapes of icicles and trimmed in gold. It looked as if it had arrived here from the ice queen's palace in Narnia.

The pristine white rug beneath the tree seemed like a blanket of new-fallen snow. Lucy raised her tail.

After we left the District, we presented ourselves in a state of panic at a veterinarian's office and left there with a kind of doggy diaper. This device wrapped around Lucy's back end. There was a place where special dog Kotex could be emplaced. And there was a hole in it for her tail. This solved the problem of the dripping for the moment. But it did not address the other issue, which was that our dog Lucy was now a *Love Machine.*

It was impossible to walk the dog anywhere without other dogs— male ones, I should say—presenting themselves and saying, *Hey, babe, ya wanna boogie?* Before we left D.C. we'd tried to walk Lucy across the National Mall, from the Lincoln Memorial to the reflecting pool—

but we'd had to beat a hasty retreat when a pack of strange dogs appeared, each one ready to go.

"We need to get out of here," I said to Deedie. She knew what that meant.

We got ourselves back in the car (we were driving Deedie's Honda Prelude, an extremely hot sports car with the kind of headlights that popped out of the hood like a pair of eyes suddenly opening upon the world) and drove north. Our plan was to go as far as we could the first night, hole up in a motel somewhere, and then finish the drive to Maine the next day. But first, we had one more stop to make.

My first novel, *The Planets,* had been out for six months now, and I was still struggling with the sequel, *The Constellations.* I figured that one more research trip to the town where those novels were set, Centralia, would help jump-start my writing. Centralia was a town in Pennsylvania coal country, not far from where I'd grown up, where a mine fire had been burning out of control, underground, for twenty years.

And so it was that Deedie and I and our menstrual dog pulled into Centralia on a day in late December 1991 and parked just next to the Odd Fellows Cemetery. The day was cold, and mist and fog hovered in the air. Smoke from the mine fire rose from boreholes at the graveyard's perimeter.

A huge sign in leering red letters stood next to the cemetery. MINE FIRE IS OUR FUTURE, it read.

It had been a half dozen years since I had last been in Centralia, and in the intervening years, the underground fire had continued to erase the town. Now, it appeared as if the strategy had become to put out the town rather than the fire. Residents' homes were bought out and then razed. There was block after block where there were driveways and sidewalks but no houses. One or two diehards remained in town, but on the whole the town looked ghostly and forgotten. Smoke from boreholes drifted through the winter air. One road was completely closed off by sawhorses and police tape; a gaping fissure erupted in its midst.

My novel, *The Planets,* had a wicked glee in its heart, which is no surprise given the fact that I'd written it during the first year of my marriage, a time when I was just about as happy as I'd ever been in my life. But it also had a fundamental melancholy at its core, and in this I saw no contradiction. I think my work as a writer would always be doomed by the way the comic and the horrific were juxtaposed. *The New Yorker* had said that I was "wacky," but I never felt that way. "You know, your problem," my friend Richard Russo would say some years later, "is that you think it *is* realism."

Maybe that was my problem, my inability to separate the tragic from the absurd—but then the condition that I'd been carrying around in my heart since childhood almost guaranteed that I'd see the world in those terms. For the moment, I'd convinced myself that the battle was done, my cosmic dilemma at last resolved by the all-encompassing love of the woman I had married. The fact that I still, on occasion, woke up in the middle of the night hearing a soft, insistent voice whispering, *You are still not you,* did not deter me from my optimism or my hope. But this voice did make it clear—had I chosen to pay it any attention—that the ground on which my joy rested was no more firm than the earth of Centralia, Pennsylvania, where a fire ignited decades ago still burned, a little hotter each year.

We walked up into the Odd Fellows graveyard with the dog, Deedie and I. It was twilight, and snow was gently falling. On every side of us were the graves of Centralians, many of them surely men and women who had spent the majority of their lives belowground.

Lucy growled softly, and the hair on her back rose up and her tail pointed out straight. We followed her gaze. There on the other side of the graveyard was a large man in a long gray coat. He was moving toward us in slow, lurching steps. His hands were clenched in fists.

"Jim," said Deedie, grabbing my elbow. "What is that?"

The dog growled again.

I wanted to tell her something like *It's just some guy.* But it *wasn't* just some guy. To this day I don't know what it was we saw, although the figure was reminiscent of something out of a horror film. The tattered man staggered toward us, his face hidden by a woolen cap and scarf. The scarf blew around in the cruel winter wind.

Deedie and I looked at each other, and then without saying anything further, we turned around swiftly and began to walk out of the cemetery and back toward our car. I looked back as we walked down the hill. The man was still coming.

We got ourselves into the Prelude, and we took off down the road. The lurching man came out of the cemetery gates and stood in the road behind us and raised his arms, as if trying to cast a spell.

Lucy was still growling as we drove off.

"Well," Deedie said. "That was fun."

We drove north through coal country. Our plan was to pull into the first Howard Johnson's that we saw, but the night grew darker and we saw no signs of life. I'm sure that we just took a wrong turn—or a series of them—but to us it seemed as if the mine fire that had begun beneath Centralia had now spread throughout my home state, leaving nothing but this one dark road. I watched as the needle on the gas tank slowly leaned toward empty. The snow came down.

A voice in my heart whispered, *How much longer do you intend to remain content?*

At last a neon sign flickered out of the night. There, surrounded by a healthy population of automobiles, was a tavern and a small motel.

It didn't take long for us to see, however, that this was not the Four Seasons. I would have estimated their total number of seasons as one at best. The main attraction here seemed to be the bar, in which huge dudes in leather played pool while a band performed country music in what sounded like two different keys, a half-step apart. When we asked the woman behind the bar for a room, she asked us how long we wanted it for, as if it were unusual for patrons to stay an entire night. She handed us the keys with a look that said, *Don't get your hopes up.*

Our hopes were modest indeed as we drove around to the back of the tavern. There things seemed a little quieter, at least at first. There were no lights on in any of the other rooms. Deedie and I unloaded the car and the dog, got ourselves into the bed, and closed our eyes, holding on to each other for dear life. The dog slept at our feet.

Sometime during the night, we heard a scratching sound on the door. It was Deedie who heard it first. "Jim," she whispered to me, "wake up."

"Hunh? What?" I said, emerging from a dream in which I was somehow back at the graveyard in Centralia. I thought I smelled smoke.

"There's something," she said. "At the door."

Lucy raised her head and growled. We'd changed her K-9 Kotex before settling into bed at the One Season that night, but it was hard to know how long ago that had been. The scratching sound on the door came again.

I pulled the curtain aside to see a large German shepherd standing outside our door. He looked at our room with a sense of fierce entitlement, like *Let's not have any of your nonsense; let's just open up, shall we.*

Incredibly, a moment later he was joined by another dog, some kind of shepherd/mastiff mix. He barked. *A love supreme. A love supreme.*

Lucy looked at us and then back at the closed door, upon which the first dog was scratching again. It was no mystery what was happening. The locals were answering the call.

Now the parking lot outside our room was filled with the roar of a motorcycle. It was the unmistakable *ta-pocketa-pocketa-pocketa* of a Harley, soon to be joined by another, and another. We heard voices, loud ones, guffawing and swearing. Headlights flashed against the curtains of our room. Another dog barked, a third creature having apparently joined the first two at the party in the back of the One Season Motel.

"What are they doing?" Deedie asked me, and I didn't know what to tell her. My theory was that the tavern had finally closed down, and the bikers were now assembling for a final debrief following last call. Where all the dogs were coming from, I couldn't say. All I knew was that the hormones of our dog were acting as a kind of lighthouse, guiding to our door every last sleaze-dog in the Alleghenies.

The trio of doggos barked more insistently now and with what sounded to me like more fury. *A love supreme, a love supreme.* The bikers revved their engines. A bottle smashed on the pavement. Deedie looked at me, her English-professor husband, with a sense of late-dawning disappointment, as if it were occurring to her only now exactly how little use I'd be if it came to a fight.

"What's going to happen?" Deedie asked, and she pulled on my elbow insistently. "Jim," she asked more urgently now, "what's going to happen to us?"

Athough we failed to die that night, Deedie's question continued to haunt me as the years went by. I did my best to protect my wife from the cruelties of the world, although I suspected, from time to time, that some of those cruelties lay not outside of our door but in my own heart. I thought that I was protecting her by keeping my mouth shut about my most private sense of self, but keeping a secret, especially one as atomic as the one I held, is rarely a way of protecting anyone. Like so many men, I figured that the best way to deal with trouble was to keep things locked down in the hole. It had got me this far. But I began to wonder if I could keep my silence forever.

I thought about the men—and women—that I knew and wondered how many of them, like me, bore a profound burden in secret. It made me think about my parents, whom, like all children, I'd always thought of as authority figures, as a couple who had a clear sense of what they were doing. And instead considered, for the first time, whether they had been just as clueless as I was now.

I doubted it, though. My father seemed to have something in his veins that I did not, something that enabled him to change the oil in his car, to steam the wallpaper off the rooms in our old wreck of a house, to disassemble the place's old windows and replace the chains and counterweights. Now, as I attempted to imitate him—and other father figures—I wondered whether Deedie could tell how little I understood the role I was trying to play.

I mowed our not insignificant lawn with a John Deere tractor. I sat on that thing for hours, moving around and around in a counterclockwise circle, my ears thrumming with the noise, my brain gently vibrating in my skull. I tried stripping the wallpaper in one of the rooms, but because our walls were cheap drywall rather than the plaster that had been the foundation of my family's house, the wallpaper just tore off some of the drywall beneath it as it peeled, leaving a surface that, despite my best attempts at spackling and sanding, never really appeared smooth. Other manly jobs fell to me as well— the changing of lightbulbs; the shoveling of snow; the putting up and taking down of screens. I didn't object to these tasks falling to me, since I knew that someone had to do them and that that someone might as well be me. But I feared that my fundamental uncertainty about my identity, which even now I tried to keep hidden from everyone and my own self not least, bled over into even these small mundane chores. And because of this, so many tasks I attempted to perform ended in monumental, almost operatic failure. I purchased a snowblower at Sears, for instance, and when I got it home, I saw a tiny pin fall out of the thing, a pin I learned later would render the entire thing nonfunctional. And so, when I brought the whole contraption back to Sears the next day, and they loaded a completely new one into the back of my SUV, I figured I'd solved this problem. Until I hit the gas, and the snowblower rolled backward in the storage area of the car and *crashed through the rear window of the car.*

Or: We had our septic system in the house replaced at great cost and inconvenience one summer. Except that in digging up the yard, the septic tank people somehow managed to sever the electric line that ran toward the well, thus cutting off the water supply. And also somehow sever a pipe in the perimeter drain that thus made our basement flood with knee-deep water after every rain, water that then seeped into all of our files and precious keepsakes, including Deedie's mother's watercolors, which had been stored in the basement as well.

Like Hermey the Elf in the stop-motion *Rudolph the Red-Nosed Reindeer,* who is unable to make a simple Christmas toy without disaster, I kept thinking of a mantra that explained why everything I touched so often turned to shit. *Just not happy in my work, I guess.*

But then I would remember the moments I'd seen through my own father's veneer. There was the time, for instance, when he'd propped a ladder against a tree limb, climbed to the topmost rung, and cut through the limb with a hand saw, only to have the ladder crash to the earth as the limb it had rested against fell to the ground. It was like the kind of accident that would befall a man in a cartoon—although the arm that my father broke as a result was real enough. Then there was the time he was mowing our lawn in Newtown Square and he ran over a yellow jackets' nest with the lawn mower. He'd wound up in the hospital after that disaster, all puffed up like a Thanksgiving parade balloon and bearing a newfound vulnerability to bee stings that he would suffer from the rest of his life. Clearly there were moments when my father couldn't quite pull off the man business either.

It made me wonder how many men—and women—in this world don't have a clue what they're doing, are only going through the motions of what is expected of them because they don't see that they have any choice. Oh, I'm sure there are men who really feel like men, and women who really feel like women, in this world. But I begin to wonder whether they are, in fact, an eccentric minority, like some marginal cult that exists on the fringes of town. How it is that the rest of us have become convinced that, in order to be happy, we have to act like them is beyond me.

Maybe this, too, was at the root of Lucy's disappointment. *It's bad enough that you took me off to a place that is not a pig farm,* she seemed to be thinking some nights when she gazed up at me resentfully. *But you're just a fraud.* It was hard for the dog to believe that no one else could see what was, in her opinion, so obvious.

It was hard for me sometimes, too.

One day, Deedie came into the bedroom with a pregnancy stick. Lucy raised her head. There were two lines on it.

One of our baby books suggested that the best way to make sure a dog accepts a newborn into the life of the family is to open the dog's heart using the language of smells. Specifically, it suggested we bring a soiled diaper home from the hospital in advance of the new arrival. The dog was supposed to smell the diaper and in so doing understand the shape of things to come. I guess it was like the dog equivalent of hearing an overture at the beginning of a Broadway musical, in which all the songs are introduced, so that when these same tunes are sung onstage later in the drama, they already feel familiar.

Zach, our first child, had a difficult birth. I sat at Deedie's side in the hospital, afterward, as she attempted to nurse. I told her that I loved her. Deedie looked at me with an expression that suggested she also loved me but that at that exact moment she wouldn't have ruled out smothering me with a fluffy pillow. At the end of that day I changed my first diaper—a process at which I would later become so adept that I took on the moniker of Diaper Master. When Deedie and our child fell asleep at last, I snuck out of the ward with the used diaper secreted in my day pack.

I got home that evening and was greeted by Lucy, who had been sleeping under the piano. "Lucy," I sang out, "I'm home."

Why do you always say that?

"It's from a TV show," I explained. "It was on when I was a kid."

You've said that before. I haven't seen that show.

"*I Love Lucy,*" I went on. "It was pretty funny."

I have no interest in television.

"Okay," I said. "Fair enough. Hey listen, I got something here for you."

I am hoping it is a freshly slaughtered corpse.

"Jeez, that's kind of, uh, specific, isn't it?"

We like what we like.

"No, well, listen, what I have for you isn't that. But I think you'll think it's in-ter-est-ing! Here. Smell this!"

I placed the soiled diaper on the kitchen floor. Lucy came over and gave it a snuff.

Dogs have approximately three hundred million olfactory receptors in their noses, compared with about six million in humans. Which means that whatever we smell, dogs experience that same aroma multiplied by fifty. I could smell the soiled diaper from where I stood, even with my mere six million receptors. What was Lucy smelling? I wondered. What vision of the future was now made clear to her, given the intimate relationship between dogs' sense of smell and their ability to build a world?

"Well," I said. "What do you think of that? That's something, right?"

The dog looked up at me, absolutely unimpressed. *You had a baby. I know about it already.*

"Okay," I said. "But now you know the smell!"

I've smelled babies before. I don't like them.

"Okay, but you've never smelled this specific baby before."

Specific babies, the dog said, *are the kind I like least.*

Days in a house with children grind by like glaciers, but the years rush by like wind. Our second child, Sean, was born in 1996. Lucy wasn't impressed by him either. Some mornings, we woke up with the whole family asleep in the bed, all four of us softly snoozing in a pile. One day I rose, part of this mound of damp, snoozing Boylans, and saw Lucy standing in the doorway with a look of disapproval. *Evah time I look up,* the dog observed, *you're in heyah with these creachas!*

"But you have to admit this is pretty wonderful," I said.

You people. You act as if nobody ever had a baby before. You act as if you invented the whole fucking business single-handedly.

"I don't see why you have to be so disapproving and unhappy all the time. We do everything for you! Feed you! Take you for long walks in the forest!"

You think that's what I want?

"I don't know, you tell me. What do you want?"

The dog sighed. Was it not obvious? *I want to go back to the Bacon Farm, where I was young, and there were pigs, whom I loved.*

Deedie opened her eyes, looked around the room. She saw our children tucked up asleep between our two warm bodies. "Who were you talking to?" she asked.

Our son Zach wrote a paper for school. Its title was "Our Dog Hates Us."

Zach, being fundamentally generous and sweet, took Lucy's disdain more personally than the rest of us. He had a well-established idea of what his family should be, and a happy, adoring, floppy-eared puppy dog was part of it. Instead, he had this resentful, disappointed Kennebec Valley Flycatcher. Sometimes, at the dinner table, he'd suggest we get *another* dog, a suggestion that Deedie was quick to shoot down. "We have our hands full with Lucy," she said, although it was fair to note that as the millennium drew to a close, the dog was slowing down. Now, when we arrived home, she didn't even raise her head to express her disappointment.

"We could get a coonhound," said Zach.

"Pugs are cute," said Sean.

"I've always wanted a bloodhound," I suggested, and everyone else groaned. "What?" I said.

"They are very drooly," noted Sean, who spent a fair amount of time reading informative picture books about dogs. Twenty years later, he would attend graduate school at the University of Michigan, in order to learn—as he explained it—"how to build robots that go into space."

A few weeks after Zach wrote "Our Dog Hates Us," he went into his bedroom to find that Lucy had taken a dump there. *In his bed.*

By this point, it was no longer such an easy thing for Lucy to jump up into beds, but she'd decided to put in the effort in this case. It was possible, as old age slowly crept in, that Lucy feared her deepest feelings about our family might somehow have remained unexpressed. But now she had made them clear.

Dogs aside, I've been in love only four times in my life: Shannon, London Donna, Rachel, and my wife, Deedie. I don't know whether this is high or low, but I do know that four feels good. Really, if you think about it, I have been lucky to have been in love at all.

In 1992 I sent an autographed copy of my first novel, *The Planets*, to my old girlfriend London Donna. It's one of the nice things about publishing a book—sending a copy to everyone who ever doubted you, as if to say, *See? Maybe not such a loser after all!*

Ten years later, Shannon, the girl I'd loved back in high school, went into a used-book store in Brooklyn. She reached out to one of the shelves and picked up a copy of *The Planets*. When she got it home, she looked at the title page. There was the signed inscription, from me to London Donna.

Somehow, the book had traveled from London Donna's house

in Cambridge, Massachusetts, to a used-book store in Brooklyn, in time to be there when Shannon's hand reached toward the shelf. London Donna, having received the book I sent her, must have picked it up one day while straightening up the house, given the novel some consideration, and then thought: *Yeah, this? Is the first thing to go.*

Maybe I should be more brokenhearted about this—that True Love #2 tossed the book I sent her into the trash, only for it to be picked up hundreds of miles away by True Love #1—who also, as I understand, did not like it. But sometimes I think about a line from *Adaptation,* the film Charlie Kaufman wrote years after we'd been roommates in an apartment on the other side of the wall from Shannon. *You are what you love,* goes the line, *not what loves you.*

In *Adaptation* it's not entirely clear if this line is meant seriously or if it's intended as an example of the kind of bumper-sticker sentimentality that haunts Hollywood. Knowing Charlie Kaufman, I'd guess that he means it both sincerely and sarcastically all at the same moment. There is some wisdom in it, though; in the film, the dying Nicolas Cage says to his twin brother—also Nicolas Cage—that he doesn't mind having been a figure of ridicule for all of the crushes he had on people who never quite loved him back. He feels as if he had the right to love whomever he pleased; even the disinterest of the objects of his affection cannot rob him of the purity of the love he felt in his heart.

Surely there is no better metaphor for the love we have than this. Yes, if we're lucky, sometimes we have a dog like Alex, who loves us back, whose heart seems wise and full. But most of the time, at least in my experience, the dogs I've loved have been slightly mental: Playboy, with his mulish resentment; Sausage, who never loved me quite as much as she loved a bowl of beef by-products; Matt, who was indifferent to any emotion other than his own libido. Does it change the love I bore for these ridiculous creatures, that in response to my adoration they chewed on their own paws, humped the legs of Hilda Watson, took a dump in the beds of my children? It does not. It was never the love the dogs gave me that mattered; it was the love that I could give them, especially during the years of my life when I could not figure out how to express the gnarled-up passions of my own heart.

We wuff what we wuff, not what wuffs us.

I got a job teaching at University College Cork, in Ireland, from 1998 to 1999, and our family packed up its suitcases and steamer trunks and moved to the Land of Saints and Scholars, where the boys enrolled in a Montessori school, Deedie made soda bread and shopped for Atlantic salmon at the English market, and I taught Faulkner and Hemingway to the Irish. Once, at Charles Fort in Kinsale—a vast set of defensive works preserved by the national historical trust—we saw an Irish wolfhound, a dog that made all four of us stop in our tracks in wonder. It stood there with its owner—a ruddy-faced man with a woolen cap—overlooking the ocean. We had never seen a dog so large, although it was impossible for me to gaze upon it without remembering those borzois of Nancy Johnson and my long-lost days as her Water Strider.

"I wonder how Lucy is doing," I said.

Lucy was back in Maine, being tended to by our friends Jennifer and Greg, who rented our house for the year. A few months in, Jennifer wrote us that Lucy was having what she referred to as "a problem with her anal sac." She'd taken the dog in to the vet, who in turn put on a latex glove in order to investigate this realm more adroitly. As the vet set about on this mining expedition, Lucy just looked at our friend Jennifer with a sense of resignation. *Nothing surprises me anymore,* she said.

While we spent the year listening to the bands Nomos and North Cregg playing Sliabh Luachra music, drinking Guinness, and exploring the mountains of Kerry and West Cork, Jennifer Yoder was back in our house in Maine, inserting her fingers into Lucy's back end.

When we returned home after the long and joyful year away, the dog was asleep under the piano. She raised her head, her face for a single moment infused with hope. *Maybe,* she thought, *Ruben Flood has come for me at last.* It was the only thing she had ever dreamed of, and she looked up with an expression not unlike that on the ancient knight in *Indiana Jones and the Last Crusade,* who has guarded the Holy Grail for two thousand years. *I knew that you would come.*

Then she saw who it was. *Oh,* she said despondently. *It's you.*

I stood in the empty house with the package that had been delivered to me by United Parcel.

It had been a daring move, to have all these things delivered to the house while Deedie and the boys were away. What would have happened if the delivery had been held up and it had arrived a week later, after their return? What would have happened if they'd had to return to the house early, capturing me in flagrante?

Grandfather shook his head discontentedly. "Well, and if Peter hadn't caught the wolf? What then?" And if one listened very carefully, he could hear the duck quacking from inside the wolf, because the wolf in his hurry had swallowed her alive.

I turned to the dog. "I'm just going to go upstairs for a little bit," I said. "You stay here."

Lucy didn't quite understand this. *I—*, she said uncertainly. *Will be staying here?*

"Yes," I said, giving the Word of Command. "Stay."

In normal circumstances, Lucy had nothing but contempt for Words of Command. But the dog seemed to sense that these circumstances were not normal. The dog sat down and looked at me uncertainly. *I will be staying here*, she said.

"I'll be back," I said to the dog.

Lucy wasn't sure about this. *Will you?* she said.

Sometime between the moment I came home with the soiled diaper and the one five years later when the box from Frederick's of Hollywood arrived, I had lain in the bed next to my wife in the middle of the night, my eyes wide open. From her side of the bed came the sound of my beloved's tender-taken breath. I stared at the ceiling. Once more, a voice said, *You are not you.*

I replied, *Shut up*, as was traditional.

Was it that night that I slipped out of bed as Deedie lay sleeping, slunk past the nursery where baby Sean dozed fitfully, crept down the stairs past the room with the cowboys and horses on the walls where young Zach dreamed? I went into the dark kitchen. It was illuminated by moonlight. We had a collection of knives, all arranged in a holder made of butcher block. They were not sharp.

Trans activist, author, and all-around goddess Janet Mock has a dog named Cleo. "People think our dog, by virtue of its name, is a girl, but Cleo's a boy," she commented after a 2014 speech at Claremont McKenna. She has used people's responses to the dog as a way of talking about binary and nonbinary identities. And asked how we can create language that includes everyone—not just men and women but nonbinary people as well.

When Janet appeared on the Piers Morgan program that same year, the host gushed to her, "Had I not known anything about your story, I would have had absolutely not a clue that you had ever been a boy, a male." A clever chyron below Mock's face on that show said, "Was a boy until 18."

Janet objected to being characterized in this manner. "I was born a baby, who was assigned male at birth. I did not identify or live my life as a boy. As soon as I had enough agency in my life to grow up, I became who I am."

I wanted to mention this because—although Janet is someone I profoundly admire—my own history is different, as this book makes clear. Janet was lucky in being able to come out as herself at a very early age and to live her entire life as herself. Since I published my first memoir in 2003, and especially since I served as the co-chair of the board of directors of GLAAD for four years, I have met, I would guess, over five thousand transgender people. Many of them, especially those who transitioned early, share Janet's sense of herself and their own agency.

But I know many others like myself, who did indeed live in the world as male-bodied persons, and while it wasn't a time of universal happiness, I don't deny that the rest of the world saw me as male and that it was in so many ways a boy's—and later a man's—life that I lived. I knew the truth of my soul in my heart all along; my awareness that I was female is one of my earliest memories, along with a subsequent shame and an awareness that whatever my truth was, it was something I had better keep secret.

I want to acknowledge that for some trans people, my referring to the first half of my life as a time when I was a boy, or a man, is problematic. It seems to add fodder to an argument that trans women are not "really" women if they have some experience living in the world as men. It seems to undercut the argument that we are who we are and that our identities are not negotiable, or up for some sort of clever conversation about what makes a woman or, indeed, what makes us human.

It is true that the life I lived before informs the one I live now and that many of the experiences that women have in their teens and twenties are ones that I will never have. But there are all kinds of women in this world. There are women like my aunt Erna, who never had a period, and there are women like my aunt Gertrude, who had a hysterectomy at a very early age. There are women like Dolly Parton, who rejoice in femininity and sequins and sponge cake; and then there are women like my friend Laura, who can open beer bottles with her teeth.

There are an infinite number of ways to be female on this planet, just as there are an infinite number of ways to be human, and my belief is that all of them are cool. If my experience and Janet's, for instance, are very different, that makes neither one of us one speck less—or *more,* for that matter—female.

If there is room for Dolly Parton, and room for my aunt Erna, and for Janet, then surely there ought to be room for me.

I mention all of this because I admit I grow weary with clever theories about transgender people, as if our identity is part of an argument that anyone might win or lose. If you have a complex theory about gender that does nothing to reduce the suffering of a group of vulnerable, maligned souls, maybe what you need, above all, is a new theory.

Or maybe the theory that you need is simpler than the one you've been working on. You want a theory for understanding people whose lives are fundamentally different from your own? Here's mine: *Open your heart.*

Does a strategy for understanding others truly have to be more complex than that? I don't know: if you have one that works for you, I'm glad.

As for me, I'm sticking with *Open your heart.*

It got me this far.

I walked down the stairs. I had to hold on to the walls because I did not know how to walk in heels. They were size twelve.

It had taken me over an hour to assemble myself, what with the makeup and the padding and the wig. I was like a human version of a piece of Ikea furniture. I wasn't happy with the results, in the end: I looked like a circus clown, although—you'd have to admit—a very glamorous one indeed.

The problem was that I didn't really care a whole lot about being glamorous. I didn't give a shit about being pretty, and fashion itself mostly struck me as a bore, a whole language that adults had invented that was really just an overly elaborate way of judging people by their appearance. Now, here I was, walking the runway in my giant shoes and false eyelashes. My breasts were water balloons. This gave them a fairly appropriate weight and form but also created a kind of live-action drama, on the off chance they might suddenly explode.

When I arrived on the landing I saw Lucy-dog standing there at the bottom of the stairs, looking up at me. The hair on her back stood up and she curled her lip. She snarled at me from somewhere deep in her dog throat, and then she barked angrily.

I knew that bark. It was the one she used when there was an in-truder.

She put a paw on the stairs and barked again, more aggressively this time. I'd never seen her like this. *After all these years*, I thought, *I'm going to wind up killed by my own dog.*

"Lucy," I said, once more issuing a Word of Command: "No."

The dog cocked her head, uncertain. Her tail stood erect, and the hair on her back remained all bristled up.

I took another step down the stairs toward her.

Then the dog made a soft weeping sound. She wagged her tail back and forth once, then twice.

Oh, she said. *It's you.*

I sat there on the living room couch for a little bit, the dog at my feet. The couch was white with blue vertical stripes. It was made of mat-tress ticking. I wasn't quite sure what to do with myself.

After a while I decided to take a walk outside. This was a risk, be-cause dear God: What if someone saw me? And yet, I wanted to feel the sun on my face. I wanted to exist in the world. I asked the dog, "Do you want to go for a walk?"

Lucy lifted her head, uncertain. *That's what you're wearing?*

I went out the back door, past the porch Deedie and I had built, past the hot tub where on cold winter nights the two of us sat to-gether, drinking glasses of champagne beneath the stars. I walked through the squashy place in the backyard, past the place where we once had a garden, and entered the woods. There was a path that led up a gentle incline, then slowly died out. All around me were the towering, thick trees of the Maine woods.

It wasn't the same as feeling the sun on my face, exactly. But the forest was the only place I could go where I was certain I would be unseen.

Lucy stayed close to me, curious to see how all of this was going to end.

I sat down upon the trunk of a fallen tree. I looked down at my Frederick's of Hollywood dress. It was white lace with a hanky hem, really the perfect outfit for the deep woods. The curls of my long blond wig fell below my water balloons.

Lucy looked off into the distance and suddenly began to bark. She bounced once on her front paws, then tore off into the woods. "No," I said. "Come back! Lucy! No!"

But Lucy, true to form, paid me no mind. A moment later she had vanished into the forest.

"Lucy, come?"

I heard the sound of her distantly pursuing something, as well as another sound. Branches cracked beneath its footsteps. Lucy barked angrily, but whoever it was was drawing near.

Now I had a choice. It would not do for me to be discovered by this stranger, whoever he might be. We had a neighbor who lived in a trailer about a mile up the road, and her property backed onto this same stretch of the forest. I'd never met her, but she was said to have a troubled teenage son who'd been expelled from the local high school. I didn't know his name, but I was pretty sure he wouldn't take well to running into me in full drag in the forest, assuming that drag was the proper name for it, which it wasn't.

"Lucy?"

I felt my heart beating in my throat. I could run back to the house, I guess, but then that would still leave a loose Lucy. And it wasn't a simple matter of going home, ripping off all these clothes, taking off the wig, and scrubbing off the makeup. I mean, yes, I could do all that, but removing eye makeup took a while, and often there was residue anyway that I was certain others could discern. Worse than this, of course, was the residue that was invisible, the kind that stayed on my heart. Every time I'd gone through this process, this transfiguration, a little of me remained, invisibly, in the world in which I'd traveled.

When I was young and crossed my eyes, people would say, *Be careful, they'll stick that way*. This turns out not to be true, when it comes to eyes. With gender, though, it kind of is. At least for me.

The heavy footsteps drew near. Now there was no sound of Lucy at all.

And now, incredibly, a moose lumbered into view. She was chewing something in her mouth. The large, ungainly creature stepped toward me and then paused. She looked me in the eyes and froze.

We both had the same thought: *Wow, you're really hideous.*

The moose stood there for a while, reviewing the situation, chewing her cud. We spent a long moment together, the lady moose and I. She was actually kind of lovely, if you looked at her with the right pair of eyes.

At last she turned and walked with equal measures elegance and awkwardness on into the forest. I watched her go. The heavy footsteps cracked deep in the woods long after the moose herself was no longer visible.

I was alone again, my heart still pounding. A sound escaped from my throat, a sound almost like laughter, but then my throat closed. I sat down on the fallen tree and felt the tears rushing to my eyes. I began to sob, about as hard as I had ever wept in my life.

I don't know what to do.

I thought about the note that I might leave.

My sweet family. I am so sorry.

Oh, how the tears rolled down and the darkness closed in. I don't know how long I sat there, a big damp, miserable, ecstatic, hopeful, doomed thing. A strange flower in a dark forest.

And then, out of nowhere—Lucy-dog was back before me. She looked at me uncertainly, put a paw upon my knee. *Hey,* she said. *Snap out of it.*

I looked up at her, my face wet. You don't know, I told the dog. You can't fucking imagine. I'm going to lose everything.

The dog thought this over. *Not everything,* she said.

No?

The dog rested her soft face in my lap. I was fairly sure she was mistaken, but I was willing to hear her out.

Some things you will keep.

We sat there in the forest together, the sun flickering through the needles. Not far away was the stream that came down from the hills and flowed past our house. I could hear it trickling over the rocks. Its waters were so dark.

VII

Ranger, 2018

He's telling me a secret, said Sean.

Lucy was not wrong when she predicted, *Some things you will keep.* By my late fifties, I'd been female for almost two decades. I'd changed my college, my gender, and my byline. But I'd kept my family.

On a spring day in 2017, we floated around the Central Park lagoon in a rowboat, my son and I. We had a couple of bottles of beer in the boat with us, although he was reluctant to open them. "Isn't it illegal?" he asked. "An open container?"

"Well, you know me," I replied. "Always the dangerous revolutionary."

My son laughed. By the age of twenty-three, Zach had emerged from Vassar College a gentle, witty, generous man, fond of acting, and of cooking, and of *Dungeons & Dragons,* and of his girlfriend, Emily.

Now, as he rowed me around the lagoon, I looked upon him with love. He reminded me of a version of my own younger self at that same age, except—as I said to Deedie now and again—"without all the tears." If he had not yet launched into the world (he and Emily were living in Washington, D.C., as she embarked on a doctoral program, and he took on a few temp jobs), I had no doubt that he'd figure out his path in time. I remembered that at his same age I had been living one floor above the S&M dungeon with Charlie Kaufman and working on my novel about the wizard who owned an enchanted waffle iron. My son would find his way eventually, I thought, and in the meantime, what we had was the blessing of a warm spring day and our love for each other.

Zach and I rowed around the lagoon until we found ourselves beneath a stone bridge with perfect acoustics. We began to sing a song by Brendan Behan, one of our favorites when raising a jar together, "The Auld Triangle," with its concluding verse about a convict's longing to dwell for a while among the women "up in the female prison."

Our voices echoed together, my son's and mine. So there we floated. A boat against the current.

For a long time it had been unclear whether our family would endure my coming out as trans. In the wake of that unveiling, I had found myself able to live more authentically in the world, to be sure. But it was also true that the old me had suited everyone just fine, and my wife not least. Finding herself unexpectedly married to a woman had not struck her as the most obvious way to improve our marriage.

It was not my mother's happiest moment either. By the spring of 2001, Hildegarde had at last found herself living a life without dogs. She'd decided to stay in our old haunted house, which seemed curious to me at first; it was such a big place just for one woman, a woman who—to be honest—really lived in only a handful of its many chambers. It was sad to think of her there, without my father, without her children, and I know there were times that she felt lonely. But her buoyant disposition, on the whole, lifted her over these moments, just as it had when she was a child and it had been her job, once again, to yank her drunken father from the pigpen.

I would often find her, when I came back to Devon to visit, sitting contentedly in a rocking chair, needlepointing, or listening to classical music on the radio, or reading the latest political biography or literary novel. When I was growing up, my friends had christened her "the Good Witch," and even now there was more than a little Glinda to her. She'd throw her arms around us and usher us toward the guest rooms with joy and cheerful serenity. Sometimes I'd wonder, Why was it that my mother seemed so deeply at peace with the world? She'd lived about the hardest, most impoverished life of anyone I knew—at least until she was twenty and made her escape from her parents' "dirt farm." She had been scarred by the turmoil of her youth, and by losing her husband so young, and by the inevitable empty nest as my sister and I headed out into the world—but she always had that Good Witch energy, as if she'd just floated down to earth on a bubble and was now happily waving her wand over the heads of those she loved.

I don't know. Maybe she was just glad, after all these years, not to have to be cleaning up after a dog she did not want. Old Brown had given up the ghost in the early 1990s, about the same time as Alex, and in the post-Brown era it had occurred to Hildegarde that finally, at last, there would be no more dogs to tend.

Her infectious contentedness might also have come, at least in part, from the Lutheran church that had now become a regular part of her life. My father, the fallen Catholic, had wanted to spare his children the gibberish of the church, and as a result my sister and I had largely been left to our own devices, as far as the eternal was concerned. But with all of us—and the dogs—finally out of her hair, my mother settled into the front pew of the St. Luke Evangelical Lutheran Church in Devon, and it gave her a tremendous sense of belonging and peace to be part of that community.

And so it was, in 2001, as I sat down to tell her, after forty-two years, that I was trans, that I felt my heart pounding, wondering whether my conservative, religious mother would find in my unveiling a final sense of tragedy, a misfortune more or less of the same degree as my father's death from cancer fifteen years earlier.

I poured her out about the strongest gin and tonic I'd ever made for anyone and I sat down and then I spilled the beans.

"I'm sorry I never told you before," I said, "but I was afraid that if I told you the truth about who I was, that you wouldn't love me anymore."

I started to cry, and the tears rolled down my face and hung there suspended at the bottom of my chin.

Hildegarde thought things over. Then, my tiny, eighty-four-year-old mother climbed out of her chair and sat down next to me. She encircled me with her arms and said, "I would never turn my back on my child. I will always love you, no matter what." And then she quoted First Corinthians: "And now these three remain: faith, hope, and love. But the greatest of these is love."

I said, "Okay, Mom, but seriously: When everyone finds out that I'm your daughter now, won't that be an embarrassment? And a scandal?"

And she said, "Well, quite frankly, yes. But I will adjust."

She wiped the tears off of my face and said, "Love will prevail."

In this prediction she was not wrong, although there were times when things other than love prevailed as well—loss, fear, guilt. As Deedie and I moved forward together it was clear that my wife was in a transition as well—from the life she had known, and in which she'd felt protected, to a new life: one that we seemed to be inventing as we went along and in which she felt very raw and vulnerable indeed.

There were times when all we did was cry, day after day, month after month. I'd come home to find her in tears, or she'd come home to find me in tears. Sometimes we both sat there in tears. It was a moist passage.

I know couples who've split up when a spouse comes out as trans, and there's no shame in this: everyone needs to do what they need to do in order to find their happiness. But Deedie and I were reluctant to part because . . . well, because we were so goddamned fond of one another, and a life apart struck us both as a life a whole lot less fun than a life together. And so we stayed together, and to the surprise of many people who were certain they knew what was best for us, our marriage improved. As I write this, we are two weeks away from our thirtieth wedding anniversary, an occasion for which I am told the official gift is pearls.

My marriage is not perfect, and as a parent I am likewise certain of my many shortcomings. In making a career out of writing so extensively about the people that I love, I've run the risk of holding all of us up as emblems of sensitivity and wisdom, which we decidedly are not. As with a lot of families, there are times when I wonder what holds us all together, and the creeping fear I have that I have failed my wife and children in so many ways sometimes still gnaws at me.

I wonder what our lives would be like if I had kept my true self hidden, and who we would all be by now.

When another friend of ours came out as lesbian in her fifties, thus upending her own marriage to her husband of twenty years, I had a brittle argument with a conservative friend of mine. He suggested that you essentially give up the right to put your own happiness foremost once you have children, that once you open that door your only job is to ensure that your sons' and daughters' lives are complete. If you're unhappy because you can't express your sexuality, said he, that's a shame. But the time to have made that choice has passed.

I took a different position, unsurprisingly, arguing with him that children get all kinds of messages from parents, and the message sent by a mother or father who exudes misery and loss is not necessarily an improvement over a parent who makes a radical decision to fulfill the needs of her own heart. I am not against the idea of duty as a virtue, but I wonder at what point duty becomes indistinguishable from repression. Life, I suggested to my friend, should be about more than the glum fulfillment of promises made before you knew exactly what it was you were promising, or to whom.

If I seemed, to our friends, like the woman who had taken the most wildly progressive stance possible toward gender, sex, and marriage, I nevertheless wondered whether I nursed a private conservatism in my heart, especially when it came to child rearing. I boasted, in print and in person, of my sons' accomplishments, holding these up, perhaps, as proof that I was not such a terrible person after all. *Look at my boys,* I found myself implying as I celebrated their relationships with girls, the grades they earned, the plays they starred in, the colleges to which they were admitted. Surely having me as a parent hadn't harmed them after all, despite what no small number of people said, both behind my back and directly to my face. *I don't care what you do, Jennifer,* the well-wishers said. *It's those boys I feel sorry for. Who's going to teach them to be men? Who's going to guide their moral character—you?*

To these critics I would often say that I had taught my children exactly what I had hoped: to be kind; to celebrate the imagination; to stand up for the underdog; to be themselves. If being a man meant knowing how to throw a fastball or how to change the oil on your car, well, then all right: in that sense I had failed. But my hope—and Deedie's, too—was that manhood meant something a little bit more than this.

In having a father who became a woman, I told people, it was my hope that I had taught my sons how to be better men.

It was a nice line. But in time, I began to wonder if it was true. Was I really guiding my sons to be their own best selves? Or did I think of them as nether versions of me, as a kind of cosmic do-over? Surely, in Zach and Sean, these two fine souls, I had finally found a way to get the boy thing right. If I had failed as a man—and it was hard to argue against this, what with the vagina—there was still one last chance, in them, to succeed. And my idea of success, I sometimes found myself thinking, was defined in shockingly traditional and normative terms. I pictured them with jobs, with wives, with a kind of societal respectability that seemed to belong more to my own father's vision of the world than my own. Surely, if anyone had accused me of this kind of thinking, I'd have denied it. *They're not here to be me,* I'd have said testily. *They're here to be themselves.* But sometimes, I suspected, a less generous sense of the world lurked not so deeply in my heart.

I remembered trying to defend my own sense of self, when I

explained to my father that with my Wesleyan degree I was going to move to New York and try to be a writer. I remembered the look of disappointment on his face; he'd wanted me to go to law school. *You're going to be cold,* he said. *You're going to be hungry.*

Well, I might be, I said. *But I'll be living my dream.*

Really? said he. *And what dream is that?*

In 2005 the family took a trip to Yellowstone. I'd been there only once before, on the road trip with Peter Frumkin, and on that occasion Peter and I had wound up getting a ticket for $75 for not being afraid of bears. There'd been signs posted at the trailhead, about how you weren't supposed to go on this path with fewer than three people, what with the bear problem; and like the arrogant young men we were, we figured that these signs applied to people who were not us, because unlike other people, my friend Peter and I were immortal.

As it turned out, the thing we really ought to have been afraid of was a forest ranger, who strolled up to us on the path and yelled at us for being stupid. Which, in addition to not being immortal, we were.

Now I was back in Wyoming, in an adventure that Deedie had planned and choreographed. She and I and the boyos—then nine and eleven—had landed in Jackson Hole, spent a day white-water rafting on the Snake River, then stayed at a dude ranch in Idaho, just over the park's borders. One day we went fishing for cutthroats in Yellowstone, and through a series of unfortunate accidents, Zach wound up with his belt stuck on a hatch on the floor, as Sean and I piled on top of him, as the boat we were in scudded up and down on the waters. We all bounced around like a paint can in a hardware-store mixing machine, and every time we thought we'd escaped the melee, another set of vibrating waves made us collapse upon one another. In later years, this event was immortalized as "the pig pile on the poop deck," a moment of family history that I think of as the time when the four of us may have laughed the hardest in our lives.

On that trip we spent a fair amount of time trying to figure out what kind of dog to get next and what its name should be. Lucy had died just the summer before.

"Bloodhound's nice," I noted.

"Jenny, please," said Deedie. "The drool."

"But they're so wrinkly!"

"If we get a bloodhound, I'm moving out," said my wife, and it was not lost upon me that my wife, who'd decided to stay with me throughout a change of gender, nevertheless considered a bloodhound a total deal breaker.

"How about a pug?" said Zach.

"Let's get a rescue dog," said Deedie.

"I want a puppy," said Sean.

"Black Labs are smart," said Zach. "Blind people use them for guide dogs."

"I'm not blind!" I said this, although it was also true that my cataracts were getting worse, not that I knew this at the time. To me it just seemed as if the rooms I was occupying were, over time, growing slowly darker.

For the mid-Maine *Morning Sentinel* I had written a lachrymose column about the demise of Lucy that appeared on Mother's Day, a short piece about how she never came when she was called and how she appeared to kind of hate us.

A very nice reader wrote me to say, "Someday, when you meet your dog in heaven, you'll call her and she'll come."

I thought that was very nice, even if extremely unlikely.

We were at a Mexican place in Jackson Hole called the Merry Piglets the night I turned forty-seven. I was drinking something called a Big Pig.

"Krypto'd be good," I said. "You know, like Superboy's dog?"

"How about Merlin?" Sean said.

"Or Scout?"

"Krypto's really good, though," I said.

"Krypto's stupid!"

"I always wanted a bloodhound named Flash," I said.

"We're not getting a bloodhound," Deedie said. "We discussed this."

"We could *rescue* a bloodhound," I said.

"Say!" my wife observed. "Have you ever considered living by yourself in a van down by the river?"

"I like Ranger," said Zach. "If we got a pug, we could call it Ranger."

"Scout'd be a good name for a husky," said Sean.

And so on.

On the third of July that same summer, we went to the kennel to pick up a puppy, a black Lab. After the negotiations in Yellowstone, we'd settled on three possible names for the dog—Scout, Ranger, and Merlin. Sean said we should see what the dog was actually like before hanging a name on him.

We'd had the dog for a full two minutes before the four of us looked at each other and said, more or less simultaneously, "Ranger."

The next morning was the Fourth of July, and at 5:00 A.M. there was this strange howling in the bedroom. It took me a moment to figure out what it was.

Then I picked up the puppy and carried him outside and sat down on the banks of Long Pond. At my side was the small black dog, pink tongue hanging out of his mouth, tail wagging.

"Good morning, Ranger-dog," I said. I was not blind, but as we watched the sunrise together, I tried to imagine all the places this dog might guide me, in the days that lay ahead.

The day after that, the four of us were in the kitchen when the puppy squatted down, as if to pee upon the floor. I scooped him up and ran with him outside—but somehow in my hurry I tripped upon the stairs that led from the deck to the lawn—and suddenly found myself hurtling horizontally toward the ground. The three-month-old puppy fell out of my grasp, and he traveled through space, rotating gently, until he landed. I crashed into the earth a second later, right on my rib cage.

A moment later the members of my family rushed outside. There, at the bottom of the stairs, I lay on my side on the ground. Ten feet beyond my corpse was the puppy, whimpering softly.

Deedie, Zach, and Sean rushed past me to the puppy.

"Is he okay?" Deedie shouted.

"Ranger, are you all right?" the boys asked.

I lay there like a dead thing. "I think I'm okay," I said. "Don't worry."

"Don't worry, Maddy!" said Zach, perplexed. "Ranger's fine!"

Maddy was the name my children had come up with for me—their combination of Mommy and Daddy. Zach had a classmate named Maddy as well, and he'd noted that "she was very nice." And so I became Maddy. They still call me that.

Sean, at the moment of this coinage, had noted, "Or we could call you Dommy."

But Dommy didn't stick.

Years later, when I asked my children about their memories of the time when Ranger joined my family, the very first thing that came to mind was "that time Maddy threw him like a football."

I lay there on the ground, wondering if I'd broken anything. "Deedie?" I said. "Sean? Zach?"

Someday, when I meet my family in heaven, I'll call them and they'll come.

Our family survived my transition, but there were times when I worried about whether the love we had for each other was enough to protect us from the traumas of the world, traumas that seemed to creep closer to us now that we seemed so different from everyone else in our little Maine village. The author Chris Bohjalian wrote a novel, *Trans-Sister Radio*, about a couple in a rural New England town like ours, in which one of the women is trans, and the community reacts with violence and cruelty. My friend Richard Russo says that he was certain for a long time that local cretins were going to blow up our mailbox or that we would—as happens to the characters in Bohjalian's novel—come home one day to find profanities spray-painted on the side of our house.

None of that happened, although I continued to worry. What would hold us together, if the world tried to pry us apart? Would love be enough to glue us, one to the other, if something other than love— like bigotry, or hatred, or violence—prevailed instead?

At least two things managed to bind us during the most uncertain of those days. One of them was pizza. Post-transition I'd discovered a fondness for making my own pies, and on Friday nights I tore the kitchen apart with my sourdough crusts, my homemade sauces, and the various toppings that I devised. I had one I called Downeast: a whole shelled lobster served on a sourdough crust with lobster-infused tomato sauce. Then there was Maddy's Meatsapalooza: pepperoni, sausage, prosciutto, and ham, tossed with fresh basil. There was Spongebob: sautéed shrimp served with pesto sauce and a slash of sriracha. There was something called Gabagool, in which I placed an olive in a blob of mascarpone, covered each one with capicola, tossed sautéed fennel over the whole pie, and then streaked it with hot sauce. And once I even made something I called Quackup: shredded duck breast, feta cheese, blueberries, and radicchio.

It was one big crazy pizza party, but to be honest, there was nothing quite as satisfying as a basic New York slice—dough made with 00 flour, sauce, and mozzarella. On Friday nights, when I usually made pizza, it was not atypical for our children's friends to start arriving at the house, one after another, to take part in the mozzarella jamboree.

One time, a journalist—Harry Smith of NBC, in fact—did a story on our family and asked how it was we'd all stayed connected. My son Zach replied, without any hesitation: "We are bound together with cheese."

The other thing that connected us all, of course, was Ranger. As the dog grew, he seemed to occupy a central position in our hearts, especially that of our younger son, Sean.

I worried about Sean sometimes, because when he was very small he was given to strange rages over things we did not expect. He preferred food that was beige; he refused, on principle, to learn how to swim. One morning before kindergarten, he decided he didn't want to wear pants to school, and the ensuing argument concluded with tears and shouts, both his own and those of his parents.

I wondered about him as I lay in bed at night, sometimes, blaming myself for whatever dark trouble might lie in his heart. It was a conversation I'd have with myself over and over again in the decades to come, one that to some degree might echo the fear that divorced parents have with themselves whenever something bad happens in their child's life. *Whatever is wrong,* I'd think, *is because of me, and what I did.*

His hardest year was probably 2005, fourth grade, when there were a few weeks he said he didn't want to go to school at all. In the mornings Sean would lie in his bed, tears rolling down his cheeks and onto the pillowcase. *It's my fault,* I'd think again. *I have become myself at last, but at the expense of the people I love.*

Having me as a parent may not have made things easier for him, but by the time he arrived in adolescence we had a better understanding of what Sean was up against, namely, his own large brain. What he hated about school was how insultingly simple it was. When he finally had the opportunity to take accelerated classes—honors classes in physics, advanced cell biology—the cloud lifted. He went off to engineering school; after graduation he headed to grad school in Ann Arbor, where he learned more about the business of sending robots into space. Music helped, too: he played the French horn and the trumpet and the piano and sang. His high school music assembly ended with him playing David Bowie's "Space Oddity" on the piano, a triumphant performance that left everyone stunned, his parents not least. Was this the same child who, twelve years earlier, had declared with such fury and anger that he would not be wearing pants?

Years later, he explained why he had spent part of his fourth-grade year weeping in bed. *Because it was so boring. Because my teacher treated me like an idiot.*

You mean, it wasn't because of me? I asked.

You? said Sean. *Why would it be because of you?*

The only thing that could raise Sean's spirits during his hard years was Ranger. He'd come home and throw his backpack on the floor and throw his arms around the dog. "Ranger," he'd declare in the same tone of voice you might use to say, *These three remain.* The dog leaned forward to lick Sean's ears, and my son nodded, as if once again he and the dog were having a conversation in a language known only to themselves.

My memoir of trans experience, *She's Not There,* came out in 2003 and plunged me, almost overnight, into a public life that neither I nor my family was particularly well prepared for. I felt awkward talking about something so personal in such a public way. But it felt like good work to be doing. I appeared on *The Oprah Winfrey Show* four times, Larry King, a Barbara Walters special. I served as the chair of the board of GLAAD for four years, the first trans person to do so. During my time as a public person, transgender issues moved from something obscure and baroque to—on a good day—something more familiar. Sometimes I tried to shield my family from the spotlight I had put upon us, but there were other times when everyone had to grit their teeth as a camera crew circled around our dinner table, capturing us for posterity as if recording a glimpse of the elusive giant squid in its murky and rarefied depths. When my second memoir, *I'm Looking Through You,* came out, Deedie joined me on *Oprah.* When my third one, *Stuck in the Middle with You,* was published, the two of us plus Zach appeared on the *Today* show. "I live in a normal family," he told the interviewer. "I can't think of a way life could be better."

An online newspaper ran the shocking headline SON OF TRANSGEN-DER AUTHOR SAYS "I LIVE IN A NORMAL FAMILY."

People from around the world wrote me letters. Some of them asked for help I was unqualified to provide. Other people suggested I was crazy. "You must have been mole-assed as a child," one helpful reader observed. The most heartbreaking message came from a woman in Nebraska, who wrote, "The weirdest thing about you, Jenny Boylan, is that you seem almost like a person somebody could know."

Yeah, almost.

One winter, I heard from a woman who said that she was getting an urgent message from the land of the dead for me. Would I like to hear it?

I disregarded this note and went out cross-country skiing. It was a cold day, and all the blowing snow had made deep drifts in some places, odd barren plains in others. From the top of the hill I looked out over the valley and there saw Great Pond in the distance. Ice shacks covered the lake, and a couple of snowmobilers were racing across the glittering surface.

I stood by a tree out in the midst of the course, breathing in the cold, clean air, feeling my heart beat in my chest, the wind on my cheeks.

And I thought, *What is this world? What is this life?*

Ranger just glanced up at me with an expression that said, *You really think it's such a mystery? You don't think the answer is obvious?*

He wagged.

A couple of days later the woman wrote me again, saying she'd gotten the message again, that it was from my father, and that it was urgent.

So I wrote back and said, *Fine. Whatever. Put him through.*

The next day I got the following:

> Jenny, I did not abandon you. I ask now only that you
> move forward with peace in your heart. Do not take it
> upon your shoulders to save the world.
>
> I am patient. I am kind. I am exploring a realm that

is magnificent in every way. It is glorious to behold and
yet there are no words to describe.

Sweetest one, you have clearly stepped into your
own. You must understand solidly that you are loved.
Know this.

I read this with exactly the skepticism you'd expect, if a person you
did not know claimed to be channeling messages from the beyond.
I'll also note that it doesn't sound a thing like my father, either, a man
without a New Age bone in his body. Most damning of all, it contained none of his signature phrases: *You bet!* and *Why not?*

And yet, for all that, as I read this message, tears welled up in my
eyes and rolled down my cheeks.

I wonder, sometimes, if my own father thought of me the way
I thought of my sons—as a reflection of himself. It's not something
we're proud of, but it's still true: we sometimes think of our children
the way Lord Voldemort thought of horcruxes—beings into which
we pour our own souls, in hopes that some version of us will survive
into the world, even beyond the moment our own candle is snuffed out.

Was that still true? Was there still something of my father in me?
What was it I had passed on to my sons? I hoped that whatever I had
given them was the better part of my nature and not the opposite.

I strapped on my skis and put on my iPod and once again headed
out into the snows of Belgrade Lakes. Ranger came with me. It was
another perfect winter day, not as cold as the one before.

I looked out at the frozen lakes. Ranger chased the wind, then
stood frozen at the edge of a cliff, staring up at the bright sky above
him. A bird flew from the arms of a tree and headed toward the horizon.

———————

We went from a one-dog household to two in 2006, after we adopted Indigo. And, in just the way that you come to see your firstborn more clearly after you have a second child, we began to have a better sense of Ranger's eccentricities after Indigo joined our family. Indigo had a passion for tennis balls, and for swimming, and developed an unsettling habit of climbing on top of the kitchen counters and rooting around in the flour container when we were out of the house. But there was one weakness that was Ranger's alone, and that weakness was porcupines. His interaction with them never ended well. We'd hear him *yelp* in the backyard, and we'd all exchange glances. It could mean only one thing.

Moments later the dog would slink back into the house with a face full of quills. Sometimes, we could pluck them out; we learned that the quills inflate with air once they're embedded, so you have to clip them with scissors before yanking them out with pliers. But unless the total number of quills was fewer than a baker's dozen, this was not an operation that could be done with any safety at home. Usually what was required was dropping everything we'd had planned for that day and driving Mr. Needle-nose over to the vet's.

On one of the first times this occurred, the vet asked us if we wanted to have Ranger neutered while he was out cold—it being necessary to knock him out with anesthesia while the quills were yoinked out, one after the other.

We'd been planning to have the dog fixed anyway, so sure, we told the vet. Let's do that.

I wondered, after Ranger got home, whether he associated what had transpired with his ill-considered attack on the porcupine. Like, was the abiding lesson of this exchange that if you stick your nose where it should not go, you sometimes end up losing your doghood?

I am fairly certain this was not the Labrador's takeaway, because the very next time a porcupine appeared in our yard, Ranger wound up with another snoutful of quills.

I will say, however, that no one, after the dog's procedure, wrote an angry op-ed to *The New York Times* cleverly asking, *Is a dog who has been fixed REALLY a dog?*

Which is more than we could say about some other people in not wholly dissimilar situations.

Our house was visited frequently by wildlife. We still saw moose and deer, a silver fox, heard the calling of loons and Canada geese. Now and again there was an issue with skunks, a misfortune that Indigo seemed particularly subject to. It was as if the dogs had decided to divide the animal kingdom between them, in a manner not dissimilar to the way our sons had evenly divided the world of boys between *dinosaurs* and *things that go*.

You take the porcupines, Indigo seemed to have suggested to Ranger. *The skunks are mine.*

This is something of a side note, but I will state at this time that tomato sauce is really not much of a remedy when it comes to skunk bombs. On the other hand, seeing the person you love stripped naked and pouring tomato sauce out of a can onto the head of a dog in the bathtub almost, although not quite, makes the experience worthwhile.

I did wonder why it was Ranger found porcupines such an irritant. After the third or fourth time, there surely wasn't any mystery about how these interactions would end. What was it that kept Ranger from learning the simple truth about porcupines and their quills, a truth he was given a chance to learn over and over again? Was it simply a matter of principle, like Sean and his early disdain for trousers? Or was there something deeper at work?

Could it be that whatever drove the dog to these doomed battles was love itself? Compared with other dogs I'd owned, Ranger was a more modest soul, certainly compared with Matthew or, for that matter, Playboy, two dogs that considered themselves the unquestionable centers of the universe and whom everyone else in that universe had been sent here to serve. Ranger wasn't like that—he was humble, withdrawn, diffident: in his own way, not unlike my own father.

Ranger loved our children. Each afternoon he sat by the door, waiting for their return at the hour the school bus approached.

So maybe it was just that he felt the porcupines posed an unbearable threat. They scampered into our yard with their needles pointing in every direction. All Ranger could think was, *What happens if one of the boys gets punctured? Who will they blame then?*

It would be me, he concluded. *And that's why that's never going to happen.* It wasn't that the dog was certain, somehow, that this time he would prevail. It was simply a sense of, *Well, better me than one of these children.*

In this he was not so unlike Deedie and me, or most parents, really. We find ourselves driven to all sorts of ridiculous escapades, solely because we think we're protecting the ones we love.

But sometimes the ones we love don't want protecting. Sometimes the ones we love don't understand the thing that is in our hearts. Sometimes the ones we love just look at us, our faces full of quills, and wonder why we thought that this was the way to save them, or how, in fact, we'd ever convinced ourselves they needed saving in the first place.

Thanksgiving 2017: Our children were now twenty-three and twenty-one. Indigo had been gone for a few months, and Chloe was newly arrived as our adopt-a-dog, after the death of her previous owner from cancer. She'd been part of our family for only a month, though, before we had to bunk both dogs at the bed 'n' biscuit for the holiday. Chloe gave us a lonesome look as we dropped her off, as if she'd failed us in some way and was now being returned to the dog orphanage forever. *I tried to be good,* she suggested, although I am not entirely sure this was true. In any case, Ranger led the way into the kennels, as if to say, *We got this, trust me,* and Chloe followed uncertainly in his wake.

Deedie and I then headed down to New York City, where, incredibly, we found ourselves the leaseholders on a swanky apartment on Riverside Drive. After twenty-five years, I'd left Colby College and joined the faculty at Barnard, the women's college of Columbia University. The new gig came with a pied-à-terre on the stretch of Riverside that the Columbia faculty calls "the gold coast."

The apartment had been furnished in part by the magnanimity of my friends: Tim Kreider donated an Oriental rug; a colleague at Barnard had donated hundreds of books, which now lined the walls of the place; and Link, my old friend from high school (and the former owner of poor old Moogus), had loaned me a 1905 Steinway parlor grand. In ninth grade, he and I had pounded on the thing in the wake of smoking a great big doober, playing the blues, laughing our heads off. Now the piano stood in the corner of the apartment, the lid propped open upon the tall stick. These ornate chambers resembled something out of Sherlock Holmes. *The Case of the Overrated Professor.*

Some days, as I put down the latest stack of papers to grade, I looked around this joint and thought: *Who lives here? Is it really me?* It seemed an unlikely end for the boy who had spent his days inside a cardboard refrigerator box, waiting for the members of her family to ask her riddles.

A few years earlier, I'd addressed a group of presidents and provosts of the Seven Sisters colleges, as they turned their attention to the gnarly question of what to do about transgender students (and applicants) to their single-sex institutions. It was one of those rare nights when I'd failed to barf all over the podium, and about a week later I got an email from Barnard's president, who wanted to know what I'd think about joining their faculty, maybe teaching a couple of courses in the spring of each year. Soon enough, I'd become the Anna Quindlen Writer-in-Residence, a position named after one of my favorite authors (and friends) and whom—since I was now writing regular op-ed columns for *The New York Times*—I'd begun to feel as if I were stalking. It was Anna who, in considering my experiences as both male and female, had remarked, "You're something, Boylan. The experiment *and* the control."

The only fly in the ointment was that Deedie remained in Maine, where she was responsible not only for her students in the social work program at the university but also for her clients in two local schools where she worked as a therapist. She visited New York twice a month in the heart of winter, and I'd make the voyage back for spring break, but this new arrangement did mean that we were separated for three and a half months of the year, with me in New York and Deedie stuck in the dark Maine winter with Chloe and the ever-diminishing Ranger. (Indigo, of course, had chased her final tennis ball that summer.)

At least one of my friends thought this was the best possible strategy for a long-term marriage. "I'm serious," she said. "I'd love to ditch my husband for four months every year."

But Deedie and I weren't thrilled about it.

We convened at the New York apartment that Thanksgiving because it was more or less the midpoint between the various cities where the Boylans now resided. Deedie and I came down from Maine; Sean took the train from Rochester, where he was an engineering student; and Zach and Emily came up from Washington, D.C. We didn't quite have the wherewithal to mount a full Thanksgiving feast in the apartment, so we ordered most of the fixings from Whole Foods on Columbus Avenue off Ninety-seventh Street.

Zach and Emily arrived on the Tuesday night before Thanksgiving, having driven up from D.C. As they entered the apartment, I had a fleeting thought that my son was, at last, launched into the world. He looked good, with his twinkling eyes and of course those dimples I had first laid eyes upon the moment he was born, when he first opened his mouth and cried, and Deedie, hearing that sound, just looked at me and said, *This is amazing.* He'd finally landed a job he seemed to like—being the receptionist at a community health center in the capital that aided families with autistic children. Emily and Zach made themselves at home on the couch, and I opened some bottles of beer, and the *craic* was good.

I had long wondered what the world was going to be like, once my children were grown. As I sat there, I thought, with wonder and glee, *Oh. It's going to be like this.*

Then Emily and Zach looked at each other nervously. I noticed that my son was twisting one hand in the other.

"Listen," he said, looking his mother and me in the eyes, "there's something I have to tell you."

A friend of mine told me that Shannon—my old love!—had published a book of poems. I was delighted. It was the first time I'd heard news of her in years. It made me happy that the girl I'd tried and failed to befriend so many years ago had at last published a book, had succeeded in creating complex art about the world.

"One of them is about you," he said.

Oh?

The poem was called "Being a Woman."

The poem, written in blank verse, spoke of a boy in high school who called her on the phone all the time, an incredible pest! She really hated this boy, and she wanted to just cut him out of her life entirely. But her mother had told her she couldn't be mean to boys.

I keep hearing everyone speaking about this . . . Penny. She must be a horrible—

The poem ended with the exposition that this person had come out as trans and was no longer a boy. "So does that mean," the poem concluded, "I can be mean to her now?"

Wait a minute. Wait. Wait. I'm—

I think—Wait. Oh no.

I'm Penny? Oh no. Oh no. Wait.

. . .

I'm Penny.

The day after she came out to us, Zaira and Emily left the house to go shopping. Zaira was the new name Zach had chosen, Spanish for "Sarah." Their plan was to get makeovers, see some friends, rendezvous at the house in time to receive Sean, who was coming down from Rochester by train.

Deedie and I had a long conversation in their absence, as we tried to make sense of the suddenly changed world. Given that we'd become two of the most visible symbols of support for transgender people in the country, the fact that our child's unveiling had left us with such mixed feelings was unsettling. Was it the suddenness of Zai's revelation that had unnerved us so? We'd seen no signs of an emergent trans identity all these years—but then, she herself said that her understanding of her identity had come to her fairly recently.

Unlike me, she hadn't had a sense of her gender dysphoria since her earliest memory of being alive; for Zai, the light had flicked on just a few months before. But it had arrived with no less a sense of illumination or certainty about what needed to happen next.

She was moving forward with transition.

As I sat there on the couch with my arms around my son—now daughter—I had wondered whether I was going to be able to be as good a mother to Zai as my own mother had been to me. And I also understood, perhaps for the first time, how difficult the thing was that I had asked everyone around me to embrace, when I'd come out all those years ago.

I listened as words came out of my mouth that echoed some of the least helpful things that people had said to me almost two decades before. My friend Rick had said to me, when I came out to him, "You're asking me to accept a fundamental change in the one person in the world of whom I could quite honestly say, 'I wish he would change nothing.'"

I remember how frustrated I was to hear these words spoken by one of my closest friends. Now I was saying the same thing to Zai. It wasn't that I didn't want her to be happy. It was just that I loved the son that I had.

We had known her name before she had known it herself, given it to her when she lay in Deedie's womb. Now she had a new name. We had loved her face from the day the doctor had held the child aloft in the delivery room. Soon, she would have a new face.

Our reaction to her unveiling was not what either Zai or Emily had been expecting. Gently, Emily said, "We need to celebrate Zai's courage, and be glad about the fact that she's finding her truth!" Emily, for her part, was completely supportive of Zai's transition; within the year, in fact, the two of them would be engaged.

I wanted to embrace the news with joy—wanted to embrace it with all the positivity and love that on the whole had been absent from my own unveiling back in 2000. That I found myself unexpectedly dragging my heels seemed to be revealing something to me about my own character that felt ugly indeed. What hard thing in my heart resisted the same truth in my child that I had demanded everyone else celebrate in me?

When she first told me her truth, my very first reaction to my daughter's coming out was to convulse in my chair, as though I'd just been struck by lightning.

It was probably not the reaction that Zai was expecting from me. When I think about it now, it makes me feel ashamed. But that's what happened.

And so lightning had struck twice. But when I saw the forking flash of light descend, I was the one who felt the merciless voltage of the unforgiving world. *No,* I thought, *it can't be.*

It makes me just a little more understanding of Dr. Boyer, the veterinarian, who, upon finding Lloyd Goodyear and me skulking around her farm in search of old dead Toby, refused to believe us when we told her our tender but unlikely tale.

That, she'd said in considering our truth, *is the worst story I've ever heard.*

The next day, Deedie headed down Broadway to gather the elements of our feast from Whole Foods. I, meanwhile, walked three blocks north to Riverside Church, where my pastor, the Reverend Doctor Amy Butler, had agreed to receive me in her office, high up in the bell tower of the cathedral.

Amy Butler and I had become friends almost from the day I'd

started going to Riverside, that same semester I'd first started teaching at Barnard. In each other we recognized a strange common ground, even though she was a Baptist from Hawaii and I was the transgender Verlyn Klinkenborg. But we were drawn toward each other from the start, perhaps because each of us struggled with the questions of faith and doubt, even if from decidedly different positions. Both of us wondered what to do about the parts of the Bible that seemed silly or just plain wrong—like all those instructions on how to treat your slaves, or those angry suggestions on how to murder your child, or the just plain weirdness of the tale of the talking donkey. It was this last that had severed my faith for good, decades ago. I still remembered telling my mother—if your donkey started talking to you, you wouldn't (as Balaam does to his ass in the Book of Numbers) explain the reason you are whipping him. You would, in fact, say something like "Whoa, I've got a talking donkey! *I'm going to be rich!*"

Somehow, though, I had come to embrace a faith founded solely upon the idea of love and forgiveness. If I could do just this much, I figured, it might be possible for me to look past the rest.

Riverside Church was one of the most powerful progressive churches in the country. It was from the nave of Riverside that Martin Luther King, Jr., had delivered his landmark speech "Beyond Vietnam" exactly one year to the day before he was killed. Later, Bishop Desmond Tutu had stood in the same place. Its former minister, Reverend William Sloane Coffin, had helped galvanize resistance to the Vietnam War, had supported nuclear disarmament, and had agitated for the rights of LGBTQ people long before this became a mainstream progressive belief. That its senior minister, Amy Butler, had become my friend struck me as strange and wonderful. We went out for drinks now and again in Morningside Heights, where we spoke of our children, and our love lives, and our doubts.

I rode the elevator up to her office in the tower. The tallest church tower in America, the place looked a little like a limestone version of Isengard in *The Lord of the Rings*. This, of course, meant that Amy Butler was Saruman and that I—if everything went just so—might, at the end of the forthcoming conversation, wind up entombed upon its roof like Gandalf, until my unlikely rescue by a pair of giant eagles.

"Jenny," said Amy, rising from her desk. Out the windows I could see the Hudson River and the distant horizon of New Jersey. She was wearing a minister's collar—something I'd rarely seen her in before. She spread open her arms, and into them I fell. "You are loved," she said. "You are loved by God. And by your family. And by me."

"Really?" I said to her. "How can you possibly know that?"

I sat down on her couch and burst into tears.

"Jenny," she said, wrapping her arms around me. "These three remain."

I can't say that whatever hard place there was in my heart melted completely after my talk with Amy Butler that day. But I think I began to understand then—slowly, painfully—that as much as I had wanted my children to be like me, I wanted, at the same time, to spare them the suffering that had brought me whatever dim insights I had found in this world. Being trans had been a burden for much of my life, but it was also a gift: it had enabled me to see things that other men and women were blind to. I wanted my child to be able to see the things that I could see—but I didn't want her to have to suffer in order to bring that vision about.

"People are going to say I did this to her," I said. "That I made it all look attractive. That I *made* my child this way."

"You can't make someone trans," said Amy.

"That's what I always told everyone! Who would ever live this way unless they had to? Unless the only alternative was jumping off of a cliff?"

Now it was Amy's turn to look out the windows of the tower. I wondered if far below us, in the bowels of Isengard, Saruman was breeding an army of fighting Uruk-hai. "Your generation thought of being trans as something to be ashamed of," she said. "But maybe that's what's changed. Maybe you can't judge what your child's life will be like using your own life as a yardstick. Her life will be hers. I mean—I hate to say this, Jenny, but, maybe it's not all about you? Just once?"

"Being trans has been miserable for me," I said to Amy through my sobs. "I wanted to spare them."

She handed me a box of tissues. "Because of your work," she said, "the world has changed. It won't be miserable for Zai, and for the kids in our children's generation. You helped bring that about."

"It's not what I wanted!" I shouted at her.

"I once read a book," she said, "in which the author said, 'You don't get to choose your gifts in life. You only get to choose what you do with them.'"

"Really?" I said, choking on my hot tears. "What *asshole* said that?"

"Jenny Boylan," she said. "I think it was you."

"Yeah, well," I said. "Figures."

"Jenny," she said, "you and Deedie are two of the strongest people I know." She put her finger on my forehead. "God will grant you all the grace that you and your family need."

"I don't deserve this," I said to her. "I haven't done anything to earn it."

"Jenny," she said, "that's what grace is. The gift that you cannot ask for, but can only receive."

From over our heads the carillon began to peal. I thought about climbing up into the bell tower at Wesleyan and playing "How Can I Keep from Singing" on the college bells. It seemed like a long time ago, but it wasn't.

> My life flows on in endless song;
> Above earth's lamentation,
> I hear the sweet, tho' far-off hymn
> That hails a new creation;
> Thro' all the tumult and the strife
> I hear the music ringing;
> It finds an echo in my soul—
> How can I keep from singing?

My sister's horse galloped toward the top of a hill. Matthew raised his leg and peed on the wall of my parents' house. I brought a diaper home from the hospital. Lucy lowered her head to give it a sniff.

It occurred to me that on that New Year's Eve many years ago, when Alex had raised one paw and pointed toward the ocean, it was to this moment he had been pointing.

We waited for Zai and Emily to come home, our new daughter *en femme*. Sean was also expected to arrive from Penn Station, after the long journey down from Rochester. One child would have to tell the other the news. Then, we got the news from Zai and Em that they wouldn't be home until ten. Deedie suggested that it wasn't fair for us to have to sit with the news for the three or four hours between the time of Sean's arrival and their own. I also noted that if you were going to come out as trans, it was best to do it while still presenting in the old gender. It makes it easier for everyone, I suggested.

My daughter was not impressed with this suggestion.

Instead, she simply called Sean on the phone. He was still on the train. She told him her news.

Later, when Sean finally came through the door of the apartment, the young scientist greeted us with a smile. "Hey," he said. "Is there anything to eat? I'm starving!"

"Did you talk to—your brother?" asked Deedie. "Did you two— have a conversation?"

"Yeah," Sean said. "I talked to Zai. She sounded good." He walked into the kitchen and opened the refrigerator. It was now full of turkey and mashed potatoes and bowls of stuffing. "Do we have any lasagna?" he asked.

Was it possible, I wondered, that in a single generation we'd gone from trans issues being a scandal and an embarrassment—as my mother and I had described the terrain—to something so routine and normalized that a sibling's transition was of less urgency than the need for lasagna? Could it be that this was another difference between my reaction to Zai's coming out and Sean's—that at least among a certain demographic, being trans is something you get to celebrate, rather than something you have to apologize for and provide explanations without end? I'd spent many hours—both before and after transition—trying to justify my identity, bending over backward to make it plain that I'd really had no other choice, that in the end I had done the only thing possible short of taking my own life. Now, for my children and their generation, being trans was—what was the phrase?—*just one more way of being human.* Was it possible that what was once something to be ashamed of could now become a source of joy? That, just as Robert Hunter had written so long ago, we had reached a day when *things we'd never seen had seemed familiar?*

If so, why was I so committed to the old ways of thinking, having done as much as anyone, I hoped, to try to shatter them completely?

I thought, fleetingly, of the words of Frodo as he takes his leave of the Shire. *I have been too deeply hurt, Sam.*

I tried to save the Shire, and it has been saved, but not for me.

The following summer, on the Fourth of July, Sean and I set out on a little boat. On Independence Day my little town in Maine shoots off fireworks above the north half of Long Pond, and the lake fills with hundreds of boats, floating on the peaceful waters, while overhead the heavens turn crimson and gold and twinkling fire arcs toward earth.

Earlier that morning the house had been filled with eight people, but now it was down to just Sean and me. In the run-up to this date, Zai had invited a bunch of her friends from Vassar to join her at our house, and we'd spent the long weekend eating lobsters, noodling around on the boat, climbing mountains.

On the fifth of July, Zai was scheduled to have something called "facial feminization surgery," down in Boston. It is exactly what it sounds like. Lots of trans women have it as they embark upon transition.

I had initially reacted to the prospect of my child's face being changed with sorrow and fury. I had first seen that face the second Z had emerged from the womb by cesarean section. I remembered the expression on that tiny face, shiny from creation. Now it was going to change.

Of course, I had considered having FFS my own self, back in the day when I was the one popping out of the box. I had told Deedie what

I wanted done, and she had looked so alarmed that I'd decided to let this go. I felt, somehow, that if I did not change my face, it would be a signal to Deedie that the person she loved was still the same. It was my hope that by doing just this much—or by not doing it, I suppose—I might increase the chances that our marriage would survive.

I'd reminded Deedie of this passage as the date for Zai's FFS drew near. I never knew what it was like to be attractive, I said to her melodramatically. But it was a fair price to pay, if it meant you and I could last.

She looked at me as if I were a crazy person. "I don't remember any of that," she said. "If you wanted to have that surgery, you should have just had it."

I thought, *Seriously?*

But I also thought that having never been gorgeous had never struck me as a particular loss. Anyway, most of the women I know never had that experience either—at least not if gorgeousness is measured by the metric of a little button nose. Which is not to say I don't know a lot of pretty women. But it's not their faces that make them beautiful.

Zai wanted to have a party the weekend before the Fourth to essentially bid her old face bon voyage. She'd had high hopes of amassing a dozen or so of her friends at the house for this occasion, but as the day drew near, some of them started dropping out. In the end, the guest list was reduced to three.

The day they'd arrived was a perfect summer day, assuming that anything could be perfect in the age of Donald Trump. I felt hyperaware that day of the preciousness of our lives and tried, every second of every hour, to be aware of the small gifts I had been given, in this new era in which it seemed as if so much else had been lost for good.

The night before, just before bed, I had mixed up some pizza dough. The recipe was pretty simple—all it really requires is flour, yeast, sea salt, and time.

The dough had been rising all night, and in the morning I divided it into a half dozen balls, dusted with flour. These I covered with a tea towel and let them rise again.

I made Deedie an omelet for breakfast. By our feet Ranger and Chloe looked up at us with their old, gray faces, hoping for a tidbit.

Then we got in our little boat—*The Red Wedding*—and scudded across the lake to poke our heads in at the general store and also to visit the farmer's market. We startled a great blue heron. It rose unexpectedly from the reeds along the bank.

I had once told Zaira that she reminded me of that heron. "Sometimes you think you're too awkward, or too strange," I'd said. "But then you take wing." She'd rolled her eyes at this, but I didn't mind. A lot of truths sound corny when you say them out loud.

At the farmer's market we bantered with the right-wing sausage man. Sometimes he wore a T-shirt that read: PETA: People Eating Tasty Animals. We bought some garlic scape, and some pesto, and some greens for salad.

Deedie and I headed back home and I tied the boat up at the dock. Ranger and Chloe were howling piteously, unable to believe we hadn't included them on the boat ride.

The howling had failed to wake Sean. He was home after graduating college in May and was spending the summer lolling around the lake house before heading on to graduate school in robotics that fall. There, my son would become a Wolverine.

When Sean finally woke up, we sat down together and watched the World Cup. England beat Colombia on a penalty kick. I loved spending time with him that summer watching soccer together. Sometimes I wished the games would go on forever.

It was hot for Maine—the high eighties—and I spent part of the day swimming in the lake. Long Pond is full of rocks, and I banged my knee against one of them as I swam and said, "Ow."

"Jenny," said my wife, "are you okay?"

She'd been working in the garden. There she was, surrounded by elfin mountain laurel, Joe Pye weed, penstemon, masterwort, and vanilla gorilla.

I was fine. I took a walk down our dirt road. One of my neighbors passed me on an ATV. I tipped my straw hat to him as he went by.

In the afternoon Zai and Emily and the three friends arrived, having driven up from Washington, D.C., where it was considerably hotter. There was a lot of hugging and kissing. The dogs barked at everybody. Bottles of ale were cracked open.

The young people hung around inside listening to the Decemberists while Deedie and I had gin and tonics on the porch. Then I tied on an apron and started up the pizza factory.

For dessert we ate blueberry pie with ice cream.

I cleaned this all up as the young people headed out to the dock in the dark to swim. As I wiped down the counters, I listened to the new "lost" John Coltrane album, *Both Directions at Once*, which after fifty years on a shelf still sounded shocking and new.

Then Deedie and I climbed into bed. Through the open windows we heard the calling of loons. They mate for life.

From the dock we heard the soft voices of our children and their friends. I read a little bit of Rakesh Satyal's novel *No One Can Pronounce My Name*, before my eyelids felt heavy and I turned off my light. I could tell by Deedie's breath that she was already asleep.

But I lay there for a while in the dark, listening to the sounds.

————

On the Fourth, everyone scattered. Deedie took one of Zai's friends to the bus station and then headed off to Gloucester, Massachusetts, to visit my cousin MJ. The others packed up by noon, heading toward the Boston hospital where my daughter's FFS would take place. By nightfall, Sean and I were alone in the lake house with Ranger and Chloe. As twilight came on, we set out in our boat to watch the fireworks explode above the lake. There we floated together, my son and I, as the sparks drifted down all around us.

Sean and I returned from our night lake journey to find the dogs sleeping soundly on the floor. This was unusual, given the terror that fireworks usually induced in them, but then we'd slipped both dogs some Valium. Now Ranger's paws moved gently as he chased a rabbit in some dark dog dream.

Later, I climbed the stairs to my bed—stairs that Ranger, in his old age, could no longer ascend. There were still a few scattered fireworks—crackers and chrysanthemums, time rains and jellyfish—falling on the lake, and the world seemed like a place made mysterious by noise and light and smoke. As I lay in my bed, I thought about my wife, and my children, and the long journey we had all been on together, a journey that sometimes seemed quintessentially American to me, an idealistic quest for resistance and invention. It was during a fireworks show in my hometown, back in 1987, that Deedie and I had first really fallen in love, forming some kind of unspoken agreement that night about what the rest of our lives might look like.

Now, all these years later, the memory of the porcupines—Ranger's arch nemeses—returned to my mind as I hovered on the edges of sleep.

If Ranger had failed to learn anything about the dangers of placing one's muzzle where it should not go, the same might well be said of the porcupines themselves, who, to be fair, had not concluded from

Ranger's attacks that there was any particularly convincing reason to avoid the Boylan property. Maybe it was just that they'd always emerged the victors in these skirmishes. Still, on they waddled, year after year, convinced somehow that this time things might end differently.

It made me wonder if it hurt, to have your quills yanked out, but then of course it hurt. How could it not? It was funny, I thought as I lay there listening to the soft explosions over the lake, that it had never occurred to me even once to think of things from the porcupine's point of view.

Zai and I had, over the years, developed a kind of system for dealing with the porcupines—or porkys, as we called them. Before Ranger could bite them, we'd sometimes go out into the yard with a large cardboard box, which we'd lower swiftly over the porcupine and trap it. We'd then slide a piece of plywood under the box, invert it, stuff the whole business into the back of the Jeep, and drive several miles away, where, with a fair amount of caution, we would release the porcupine into the wild. The porcupines would scurry out of the box and climb into a nearby tree and give Z and me a look, one that was perhaps remarkable for its complete lack of gratitude.

It put me in mind of a story Russo had once told me about a family whose car had broken down in the Arizona desert; when the man arrived with the tow truck, he opened the hood, stared into the car's innards for a long moment, then shut the hood and declared, "I can't help you." When asked to explain, he went on: "I fix cars. But what you've got here—is a porcupine." Apparently a porky had climbed up inside the engine while the car was parked and only now, several miles out of town, had it decided to stage its escape, puncturing hoses and fuel lines in the process. Later, as they waited for the car to be repaired, a local boy had encountered this couple's children in a diner and asked—since it was clearly the talk of the town—"Did you hear about the porcupine people?"

The child had no recourse except to state the tragic truth. "My family—my mom and dad and me. *We* are the porcupine people."

Deedie was there in Boston the next morning when Zai came out of surgery, so high from the anesthesia that she found herself glee-fully singing, "Moses supposes his toeses are roses," from *Singin' in the Rain*.

"Is she okay?" I asked when Deedie called me later to give me the news.

"She's fine," said Deedie. "The doctor said she came through with flying colors."

"I can't believe she was singing," I said.

"Yeah, well," noted Deedie, "*you* sang, back in the day."

This was true enough. They'd wheeled me into the OR sixteen years before, singing "I'm Gonna Wash That Man Right Out of My Hair."

"So—who does she look like?" I asked her. "Now that she's done the thing?"

"Well, she's kind of banged up," said Deedie.

"I know, but still—"

"She looks like herself, Jenny," said Deedie. "Who else?"

I took the *Downeaster* train a few days later to be on call for the sec-ond half of Zai's recovery, as Deedie headed back to Maine. During this stint I stayed with Zero and his wife, Jen, in their apartment in Cambridge. They owned a pug named Oscar. He was about as un-like Alex the Gordon setter as a creature could be and still be loosely considered a dog. It had been hard for me to accept Zero as a pug

owner, perhaps just as hard as it had been for my friend to accept his
old friend Jim as a woman.

But here we were in our sixties, Zero and me, taking a pug for a
walk through Cambridge as my daughter, Zai, recovered from facial
feminization surgery a few miles away. You know, the way one does.

I had asked Zero to read the chapter in this book about Alex. I was
saddened to find that it had upset him, not because anything in it was
untrue but because there were a lot of things in it that he wanted kept
in the past. "I feel like everything I say with you," he said, "I have to be
careful, or you're going to put it in some book. Is there no such thing
as intimacy? Or privacy? I mean, what about *this* conversation? Is *this*
going to wind up in some book of yours?"

"Would I do that?" I asked.

A few weeks later, Zai descended the stairs at our Maine house,
wearing a bandage around her forehead. One of her eyes featured a
truly impressive shiner. All in all, it looked as if my daughter had been
in a very serious fistfight. And lost.

"Hey, darling," I said to her. "You want me to make you some
breakfast?"

"Yeah," she said, sitting down on a bar stool that overlooked the
stove top. "I would like that."

"Okay," I said, and set to work.

I broke a couple of eggs into a bowl and chopped them around
with a fork. I put some butter in a little pan and melted it over a low
flame.

"How are you feeling?" I asked.

"I'm good," she said. "Better."

I diced some mushrooms and a red onion and sautéed them until they browned a little. Leaving this all to simmer on low, I went out to the porch and picked a few fresh leaves of basil from a big pot where they were growing. This was the same porch from which I had plummeted almost fourteen years before, when I had thrown Ranger like a football.

I returned to the kitchen and made my daughter a cup of coffee. I slid it to her on the bar. The steam rose into the air.

Ranger, now by any measure a *very* old dog, moved slowly toward us and sat down at Zai's feet. I poured the eggs into the pan. They softly sizzled. Then I added the basil and some sea salt.

Zai smiled and drank her coffee. "Hey, Siri," she said, "play Louis Armstrong." Siri complied. Soon the room was filled with the soft sounds of Satchmo singing "What a Wonderful World."

When she was six, I'd picked my child up at school one day to find her in tears. She explained that there'd been a race on the playground and that she'd come in last. "I always thought," she said, "that I was as fast as a cheetah." I'd dried her tears, and we'd gone for ice cream. I remembered sitting on a picnic bench with her as the ice cream melted down her cone and through her fingers.

With one hand I flipped the omelet in the air and caught it in the pan. Then I put some shredded cheese in the pan and folded the omelet in half with a spatula.

Once, when I was about eight, I'd stepped off of the school bus to find my mother standing in the driveway. Playboy stood by her side. She'd folded me into her arms, and I'd dissolved in tears. *I have no friends*, I'd said.

I slid the omelet onto a plate and laid it before my child. It was a woman's face, and—I had to admit—a woman's figure that I saw before me; hormones had done their work on my child in record time.

And yet, for all that, what Deedie had said was true: it was still the face I had always known and loved.

How was it that I had doubted that my child would be all right? Was it just that I wanted to stand between her and all the harshness of the world, just as I had when I was her father, just as I had tried to do in all the years since I had become her second mother? Or was my fear for her just a distant echo of the fear I had once felt for myself? Was it so unthinkable that what I had hoped for would, in the end, turn out to be true? Was it not self-evident, from all the grace that surrounded us, that my child's life would be better, where my own life had been hard?

I put a bottle of sriracha hot sauce on the counter, and Zaira squirted a squiggly red line across the omelet. Ranger lay down at her feet but looked up with his gray muzzle, hoping that something scrumptious might fall to him.

"Oh, look at that old dog," I said. I remembered the feeling of sailing through the air that day I had fallen from the porch, watching the puppy slip from my hands. "The poor thing."

Zai smiled at her dog. "He's a good boy," said my daughter.

I thought of the thing that Chloe, Ranger's wing-dog, had suggested on the day she entered our lives. *If you wanted,* she'd said, *I would stay with you.*

Those words would come back to me a year later, at the end of summer, 2019, when the vet removed the stethoscope from his ears and said, "I think you've done everything you can for him." Ranger thumped his tail weakly. "He was lucky to have such a good family."

Deedie and I could barely talk. The tears streamed down. "If you want to say goodbye to him now, we can do that," said the vet, whose name was Dr. Smith.

Deedie and I clutched on to each other. "Can we—" I said. "Can we talk about it? Maybe take him for one last walk?"

"You take all the time you need," said Dr. Smith.

Somehow we got to our feet (we'd been lying on the floor of the examination chamber next to the dog) and went outside, with Ranger on the leash. It was a sweet day in early September. There were a few red leaves on the green grass, and I thought of the picture I'd taken of Indigo before we'd lost her two years earlier, the gray paws on either side of a fallen maple leaf. A John Prine song played in my heart. *Summer's end came faster than we wanted.*

"I know we have to say goodbye," Deedie said. "But I can't do it today. I just can't."

I nodded. "Maybe we can take him home for one last night?" I said. "And make him a special dinner? Play him his favorite music?"

"Okay," said Deedie. "Okay."

We got the dog back in the car and drove silently toward home.

He'd gone downhill quickly that year. First he had come down with an affliction that Labradors are apparently susceptible to, something called laryngeal paralysis. I'd never heard of it before. It made Ranger breathe hard and heavy all the time, like he'd just run a marathon. The constant panting made him anxious, too, and he'd been prescribed Valium in hopes of calming his nerves. The indignities piled up: soon his back legs could no longer support him. It was hard for Ranger to get up, and almost as hard to lie down. He had wicked bad arthritis. He began to lose control of his nether parts, too. We'd come to consider it a good day if we got most of his fluids outside before they arrived. And solids.

One day he'd just given me a hard look. I recognized that look: I'd seen it in the faces of many of my dogs over the years: Alex, Indigo, Lucy, even Playboy, way back when. It was the one that said, *You said you'd take care of me, when the time came. You made me a promise.*

I didn't remember making any such promise, and I wonder if I'd ever have agreed to such a thing if I truly understood what I was pledging to do.

Deedie and I opened the window for Ranger on the way home. Once, he'd leaned his head out and let the wind blow his ears around.

But now he was too weak to stand.

We got him home and back inside. Deedie asked me to mix her a Manhattan, and I did: rye whiskey, sweet vermouth, a brandied cherry, some bitters. As I poured out the cocktails, she made Ranger his last dinner. Chicken and rice.

As Ranger dug into his chicken, and Deedie and I drank our drinks, she looked at me curiously. "What was that," she said. "About Ranger's favorite music? I didn't know he *had* favorite music."

Neither did I, I admitted. But I considered the question now. It was harder than I thought. What sort of music do retrievers prefer? Classical? Rock and roll? Bluegrass? For a few moments I was stumped.

Then it came to me. A moment later, his meal complete, Ranger came over to us and leaned his head against our legs, and I cued up "Ring of Fire." Deedie nodded. "Johnny Cash," she said. "Of course. The man in black."

We kneeled down and put our arms around our old friend. He had stood by our children in the mornings as they waited for the yellow school bus, and he had waited for them again when they finally came home from college years later. He had watched with patience and with love as the years rushed by with their graceful and merciless speed.

I looked at my hands, now petting his black and gray coat. They were gnarled and covered with soft age spots. Whose hands were these? I was so grateful for how full of joy our lives had been. But how had it all gone by so swiftly?

Love, sang Johnny Cash. *Is a burnin' thing.*

We'd first laid eyes upon Ranger back in 2005, the same summer we'd gone to Yellowstone and looked upon mud pots and geysers and fumaroles. Upon our return we'd gone to the kennel to get the puppy. The breeder's house was at the top of a hill, and after we parked the car, a whole pack of Labs thundered down toward us, baying. One of them was a chocolate Lab named Lady Toblerone, or Toby. Her dog teats swung around wildly.

"That's the mother," said Deedie.

We climbed up the hill to the house, and the breeder let us into the room where the pups had been whelped. Ranger was the last dog of his litter to be picked up, and as Z lifted him, the puppy licked her face. Sean leaned in close and looked thoughtful as the puppy sniffed his ears.

"What's up, Seannie?" Deedie said.

"He's telling me a secret," Sean said.

"What's the secret?" I asked.

"Maddy," said Sean, "I can't tell."

That was a long time ago.

We were reckless, capricious people, who struggled to find the words sometimes to tell each other how much love was in our hearts. We would disappoint each other, over and over, with our inability to do the right thing or to know the right thing to say. But our house would be filled with the smell of hot pizzas: Spongebob, Downeast, Quackup. Our children would lie in the dog bed by the woodstove, doing their homework as Ranger slept beside them, his paws in the air. Or he'd lift up his old gray face with an expression that said, *Don't you know how much I love you? Don't you know that this is the only reason we are here, to love one another, and to be loved?*

Why is it that what is so obvious to dogs is such a mystery to men and women?

Young Z looked at me with shimmering eyes, a distant awareness dawning, perhaps, of all the years that lay ahead.

The puppy squealed. "Maddy," Z said, "do you think he likes me?"

JENNIFER FINNEY BOYLAN, AUTHOR OF *GOOD BOY*, ON THE DOGS THAT KNEW HER BEST

In her New York Times *opinion column, Jennifer Finney Boylan wrote about her relationship with her beloved dog Indigo, and the tear-jerking column went viral.* Good Boy *uses that column as a springboard for a book that is part memoir and part exploration of masculinity and femininity, in the context of a man's, and now a woman's, best friends.*

Tell us how you came up with the idea for this book.

Dogs help us understand ourselves: who we are, who we've been. They teach us what it means to love and to be loved. They bear witness to our joys and sorrows; they lick the tears from our faces. And when our backs are turned, they steal a whole roasted chicken off the supper table.

If you want to know what lies in someone's heart, ask their dog.

Dogs also enable us to express a kind of love that sometimes we're too awkward or uncertain to share with other people. I think this is especially true for boys and men, for whom love can be particularly hard to express. As a transgender woman who began life as a boy, it's in the dogs that I owned pre-transition that I can now best understand men, and the person I once was, a long time ago.

I look upon boyhood now the way an emigrant might look upon the distant country of her birth. There are times I can't even quite remember what that country was like. But I remember the dogs: there were the mulish Dalmatians of my childhood and adolescence; there was an uncontrollable, joyful mutt named Matt during my college years; there was a deeply neurotic Labrador during my twenties, a dog who chewed on her own paws with such abandon you'd think they were a delicacy rarer than clams casino. And as a young husband, there was Alex, the Gordon setter, who knew me better, in some ways, than I knew myself.

All of those dogs helped me through a difficult life by showing me the meaning of loyalty and of love.

This is a memoir of the seven boys and men I once was, as

reflected in the seven dogs I owned at each stage of my life. To paraphrase Charlie Kaufman, *We wuff what we wuff. Not what wuffs us.*

Is there one dog you loved the most? Or is that like trying to pick a favorite child?

I've had good dogs and bad dogs, but the dog I might be fondest of is a black Lab named Ranger who, incredibly, is still alive now at age fifteen. He was there when my children were toddlers; he was there the day they left for college. My life has been a series of strange adventures and accidents—a whole universe of unexpected variables. But Ranger is the constant.

In *Good Boy*, you state: "Time heals some of the wounds that the world gives us, but not all of them, and some we keep forever. Incredibly, a few hurt more the longer ago they happened." What period of your life was the hardest to revisit while writing this book?

In my mid-twenties, I wasn't sure I was going to survive my life; I knew I was trans, but I had no idea how to come out and exist in the world. I had a relationship that was circling the drain. And my father was dying. That era came to a head when I drove up to Nova Scotia with the intention of jumping off a cliff into the cold Atlantic. And yet, something gave me hope; something helped me understand that if there is trouble and loss in this world, there is also great joy. I had a dog named Brown that came to me in the heart of that troubled time one night and put her head on my lap. This is the dog that chewed her paws. I thought of the words from scripture, slightly altered: *Whoever lives in love lives in Dog, and Dog in him.*

You've written fifteen books, including three memoirs. What makes this one unique?

I've focused on my life as a transgender woman in previous works—this time, I'm trying to focus on my life as a boy and as a young man, trying to understand what the connection is between the person I was and the woman I became. And while I understand that my circumstances are unusual, perhaps, that question—*how do we connect our present with our past*—is one that everyone asks. And one way to make peace with the past is to see what connects who you are with who you've been. For me, part of what makes that connection is love, and the love I've had for my dogs in particular.

Your writing has made such a significant impact inside and outside the trans community. What message do you hope people take away from *Good Boy*?

I understand that many trans women don't feel like they ever had a male past, that once they were old enough to achieve some agency over their lives, they became themselves. I respect that—but my own experience was different; I did live a boy's life for almost forty years, at least on the outside. I'm hoping that people will understand that having a boyhood then makes me no less female now. I'm hoping that in the story of a woman and her dogs, people will see someone very familiar, even if in extraordinary circumstances, and in so doing recognize the humanity of transgender people and feel a sense of connection and compassion.

Can you tell us what you're working on next?

Well, as a baker, I was tempted at first to write a history of pizza, entitled *A Slice of Life*. Instead, I want to write a history of the transgender movement, showing the long struggle for equality from its origins to the "Tipping Point" of the current decade. It will be a personal story, since I witnessed so much of the recent history first-hand, but it will also show the danger that our people, and our movement, find themselves in now as forces allied against us become more powerful and more cruel. I am hoping to tell the stories that will show that the arc of history is long and that it bends toward justice. I am hoping to show that with humor, and hope, and fire, we will in time prevail.

Dan Haar

Professor JENNIFER FINNEY BOYLAN, author of fifteen books, is the inaugural Anna Quindlen Writer-in-Residence at Barnard College of Columbia University. Her column appears on the op-ed page of *The New York Times* on alternate Wednesdays. She serves on the Board of Trustees of PEN America. From 2011 to 2018, she served on the Board of Directors of GLAAD and also provided counsel for the TV series *Transparent* and *I Am Cait*. Her 2003 memoir, *She's Not There: A Life in Two Genders,* was the first bestselling work by a transgender American. A novelist, memoirist, and short story writer, she is also a nationally known advocate for human rights. She lives in New York City and in Belgrade Lakes, Maine, with her wife, Deedie. They have a son, Sean, and a daughter, Zai.

CELADON
BOOKS

Founded in 2017, Celadon Books, a division of
Macmillan Publishers, publishes a highly curated
list of twenty to twenty-five new titles a year. The
list of both fiction and nonfiction is eclectic and
focuses on publishing commercial and literary
books and discovering and nurturing talent.